D1530404

FOUR CENTURIES OF
SPORT IN AMERICA

Painted from life by Chapman

Colonel David Crockett, the Pioneer Hunter

Four Centuries of Sport
in America

1490-1890

BY HERBERT MANCHESTER

INTRODUCTION BY
HARRY WORCESTER SMITH

ILLUSTRATED FROM
ORIGINAL SOURCES

NEW YORK
THE DERRYDALE PRESS
1931

PREFACE

It is the purpose of this volume to follow the history of sport in America from that of the Aztecs and Indians down through the sports of the white man to about a generation ago.

The point of view is historical rather than technical and seeks to give the story of each period with the high spots of each sport, rather than its minor details.

We have tried to include whatever the amateur sportsman in particular would be interested in, to furnish a background for a sufficient understanding of American sport in general, and to provide a point of departure for further research in regard to any particular sport.

The author's method of attacking this very diverse and widely expanded subject has been to follow the main stream of American sport from its sources, taking note particularly of where the different sports entered the main stream, of their beginnings or of their introduction from abroad, and again emphasizing any significant changes or nationally important events which may have occurred in them or have affected their character.

The history is based upon the original sources — the accounts of explorers and travellers, on old records, newspaper items, and magazine descriptions, — all from the era for which they are used. The illustrations are from manuscript miniatures, historic paintings and copperplates, early lithographs, and the wood engravings in the early American magazines, — all likewise contemporary with the period they picture. Such original sources embody the viewpoint of the people and the atmosphere of the times, and serve to give the feeling as well as the facts of the past. In some instances the only data available have been bare items in an inventory or advertisement, but even these, though they make staccato reading, help to add to the scene.

The reader should bear in mind that occasionally beliefs have changed and that the sources represent those of their time rather than of the present.

Sports, in fact, are largely an outgrowth of the life of their age. Almost every era has had its predominant sports, which have been in harmony with it. The Aztecs and Indians were so largely dependent on hunting, that it was undoubtedly their chief sport, though they had important tribal games like lacrosse. From the Indians have come most of the stratagems used in hunting, such as encircling the game, deer driving and stalking, moose calling, antelope flagging, turkey calling, and duck decoying.

When the colonists came here, they found hunting free, whereas it had been preserved at home, and there is no doubt that they learned more about hunting from the Indians than they had ever had an opportunity to learn in the lands of their birth.

The life of the wilderness developed rifle shooting until the backwoodsmen were famed as the best shots in the world.

The colonists brought in various sports that involved the use of horses, which were unknown to the Indians. Foxhunting, which had been in vogue on the estates of England, was introduced in the South and on Long Island. Horse racing, which had flourished near the big cities in England, was established in Virginia, Maryland, and near New York. Sleighing became popular in New York and Boston.

When we became a great ocean sailing race, closely related sports such as rowing and yachting came into prominence.

When the highways changed from bridle paths to improved roads, driving replaced riding as a means of transportation, and the trotter and trotting races, which had been hitherto practically unknown, were developed.

As shooting and angling became less and less everyday necessities, they became more distinctly sports, and to the skill which was in part learned from the Indian and in part developed here, were added certain ideas of sportsmanship and of the protection of game that had been evolved in England.

The massing of young men in the growing cities and colleges helped to introduce team games like cricket and baseball and football. The growth of the cities was also responsible for such indoor games as billiards and bowling, and for such products of the lower elements as prize fighting.

Out of the wars came team rifle shooting at targets, and from the Civil War especially sprang the great team contests in target shooting at Creedmoor. From the Wild West came the urge for fancy marksmanship, shooting from horseback and stunts with the revolver.

When the cities increased in population enough to furnish a steady supply of paying spectators, there followed the professionalizing of baseball and, to some extent, of other sports. With the increase of office work in the cities, came athletics as an antidote. The desire to get beyond the immediate city called into being the bicycle, which was an important adjunct of sport in the pre-automobile era. The call for outdoor exercises brought about a revival of foxhunting, polo, and tennis, and golf.

The rise of women is expressed in sport in the contrast between the much-questioned equestrienne exhibitions before the Civil War and the international and championship matches on the golf courses and in the tennis stadiums.

If such has been the outgrowth of many of the sports from their age, the influence of sports on the life of their time has been of equal significance, though it would be harder to prove.

The reader will notice two things in reading this volume: nowhere has the author expressed his opinion, being content in all cases to confine himself to the quotation of original sources; secondly, his approach to the subject has been from the point of view of the social historian rather than of the sportsman, and no effort has been made to bring out the fact that the book includes a number of items which are of first importance in advancing the knowledge of American sporting history.

It is the author's hope that American sportsmen will find in this book a sufficient education in the history of their country's sport to permit them to feel the pride in it which it richly deserves.

New York City.
August 20th, 1931.

Herbert Manchester

v

TABLE OF CONTENTS

TABLE OF CONTENTS

TABLE OF CONTENTS

TABLE OF CONTENTS

LIST OF ILLUSTRATIONS

LIST OF ILLUSTRATIONS

LIST OF ILLUSTRATIONS

LIST OF ILLUSTRATIONS

INTRODUCTION

ONLY the sun, moon, and stars (and not all of the latter), would be privileged to write a review on Four Centuries of Sport, for they alone have viewed it. But memory is given to all of us.

Do you remember 'way back? How often one older person says that to another, and how proud the one feels if he does and the other doesn't remember, and then how they both glow if they can check off together.

Now, this isn't a book for children whose furthest memory is a spanking, but it is for the mature-thinking person, and especially sportsmen who are proud of America, the *new* country which in most sports has carried all before it.

An old Chinese proverb has it that one picture is worth ten thousand words. In this work our author has not only given us pictures, but also words, so one's heart should be more than content.

I believe there are many sportsmen my age and even older who will remember some of the early methods of shooting, fishing, hunting, etc., and in the words that follow I have endeavored to show their reaction on my past calendar of sport.

The text of this book so interests me that I could write for hours, but the writer of an introduction, like a toast-master, should be brief, so I am only going to touch the high spots.

The earliest scene shows the Aztecs hunting. But their hunting was little compared with the hunting of historians for true facts about these great intellectual people, whose Calendar, weighing over twenty tons, still occupies the place of honor on the pyramid of the sun in Mexico City.

An early Aztec manuscript shows their conception of the Spanish horse. The horse meant so much to Cortez and de Soto, who explored Mexico and the southern part of North America, that in the *Horses of the Conquest* the author tells us that Cortez in his reports to the Emperor invariably put his horses first, as he no doubt did in his prayers.

Hernando de Soto brought 123 horses in 1539, and landing on the coast of what is now Florida, marched west with them and discovered the Mississippi. Henry William Herbert writes a most vivid description of de Soto's death and when I was in Natchez, Mississippi, I saw a few half-bred Indians which made me think of their forbears who Herbert tells us, "sent a messenger — an Indian runner — who when allowed to enter, crossed the chamber and flung a bundle of shafts, bound in the skin of a rattlesnake, the defiance of his tribe, upon the deathbed of de Soto. De Soto was buried standing erect as he ordered it, with a good sword in his dead hand, the polished helmet gleaming above the sunken features, and the gay banner of Castile floating like a mantle from the shoulders — the pealing notes of the trumpet and the roll of the battle-drum, and the Spanish war-cry — 'St. Jago for de Soto and for Spain' — and the crash of the volleying arquebuses might be heard, starting the wild beasts, and the wilder Indians, of the forest, for leagues around.

"There was a pause — a deep, deep pause — a sullen splash — and every torch was instantly extinguished."

> But wind me in the banner bright,
>   A banner of Castile,
> And let the war-drums round me roll,
>   The trumpets o'er me peal!
> And bury me at noon of night,
>   When gone is the sultry gleam,
> At noon of night — by torches light —
>   In the Mississippi stream.
>   —*Old Ballad*.

That was certainly a warrior for you.

Many present-day boys have been surprised at the colors of the broncos from the West, but the talented author of *Horses of the Conquest* tells us,

"I have ridden hundreds or perhaps thousands of horses descended from the horses of the conquest. . . . Gratitude to all of them; bays, browns, blacks, chestnuts, piebalds, roans, greys, whites, cream-colored with black points, duns, skewbalds, claybanks, calicos, pintos, pangarés, lobunos, grullos, zebrunos, malacaras, pampas, picazos, gateados, zainos, tordillos, melados, doradillos, overos, moros, barrosos, ruanos, rosillos, bayos, and all the rest of the affinity of colors that the Americans bring forth."

And after reading the paragraph one feels that he would need a show-card of colors to distinguish the different mixtures.

De Bry, mentioned by the talented author of this work, under the date of 1590, certainly deserves a paragraph and Baillie-Grohman in *Sport in Art* supplies it by telling us,

xvi

INTRODUCTION

"Theodore De Bry

"It will probably never be cleared up how it came that a Frankfurt engraver dwelling in a dull country town in the interior of Germany far from seaports and persons engaged in over-seas, should be the man to collect together and with the aid of his wife, two sons, and two sons-in-law illustrate and publish that famous set of the major and minor voyages to America and the Indies, comprising no fewer than twenty-five volumes in Latin, twenty-seven in German and a like number in English and French, adorned with hundreds of engravings, woodcuts and maps."

The picture showing the Recreation of Gentlemen of Virginia, in 1619, suggests that they were angling for whales, hawking on foot or horseback, chasing the red deer with a single hound and shooting with a rough type of flintlock.

It is indeed remarkable that the Indian deer drive, as described by Champlain in 1619, so closely resembled the European.

Many present-day sportsmen will be interested in the little sketch of hunting wood-hens with the aid of a dog, as shown in the scene dated 1683-1694, for many of us have treed wood-hens (our partridge) in Maine with a dog. We were taught to shoot the lower bird first, and then take the next one higher up, for if we killed the highest one first his falling to the ground would scare the others.

From Hennepin's book is taken the picture of a buffalo. What a rough coat he had; far different from the beautiful skin of a buffalo calf hanging at my Nimrod Hall in Virginia, which the Indians termed "beaver buffalo," as the hair is as soft as a beaver's, acquiring the name, as Indian legend tells us, from the fact that the mother buffalo died while calving or was killed by accident, and the young calf was taken care of by the different cows in the herd which gave the little one supper and out of kindness licked it with their tongues bringing about the softness of the coat.

What an excellent example of the influence of the Indians on American sport is their use of artificial duck decoys, which, so far as known, were never used in Europe.

The account by Charlevoix of the red fox in America in 1721 will come as a great surprise to sportsmen, and apparently establishes the fact that the red fox was native here before its introduction from England to Maryland in 1730.

1766 shows us a view of the Passaic Falls from the south and I'll wager one couldn't find today the falls near which the Dutchmen settled in 1679; but how picturesque they were. And the Indian brave at the left is shown fishing in a mighty likely pool.

How interesting to find a paragraph or two about pacers being broken to pace by hobbles in Ipswich, Mass., in 1770. This information should cause quite a stir among the owners, trainers and drivers of the side-wheelers.

1774 brings us to The Hill Tops, a new hunting song illustrated by a sketch of hounds running into a deer. That's a good name — The Hill Tops — and it belongs to fifty per cent of the sportsmen who follow the fox, for their principal occupation is to go to some highland and watch and listen to the hounds rather than follow the pack that trails Reynard.

The picture of Washington and Fairfax, is from the talented pen of F. O. C. Darley, who did such splendid work in illustrating Washington Irving's and Cooper's works. Washington's huntsman, Willy Lee, mounted probably on "Chinkling," is in the background while a slave holds the hounds in leash. Washington's Diary tells us that he often hunted with members of the Dulany family, forbears of the Dulanys of Piedmont Valley, Virginia.

There were women in sport 'way back in 1812, as the picture, A Hunter and his Wife, shows; the latter was certainly a Diana of the Chase from her attractive figure and costume, worthy of being drawn by Bartolozzi. This is an exquisite scene; the boughs and foliage of the evergreen trees are worthy of Dean Wolstenholme.

The story of the American Eclipse-Henry race interests me deeply as on May 27, 1923, just one hundred years from the time, May 27, 1823, that the gentleman rider, Samuel Purdy, rode Eclipse in the lead in the last two four-mile heats and won the $20,000, I arranged centenary exercises at his grave in the St. Paul's churchyard, New York City, at which August Belmont, Chairman of The Jockey Club, and many other sportsmen were present, and we laid a red racing jacket with cap on the gravestone, the same color as the famous gentleman rider wore in the race, and also a great bouquet of red roses.

Those who love Vermont will be glad to see the few words about Justin Morgan. Perhaps they will make a pilgrimage to view one of the few statues erected to the memory of a horse. It is to Justin Morgan at the Vermont State Morgan Farm which bears the following inscription:

1921, given by the Morgan Horse Club to
The United States Department of Agriculture
in memory of Justin Morgan who died in 1821.

In the picture of woodcock shooting in 1830 it is interesting to see that even at that time bird dogs were taught to back one another, for the black setter at the rear of the picture is evidently backing the dog on point.

Rail shooting on the Delaware was apparently identical to rail shooting on the Connecticut. Is there any better sport? In the printed text we find the old legend of rail burying into the ground and hibernating there. One thing I know is that a rail can run on the land, climb a reed, fly, and give the best warm weather sport in the world.

INTRODUCTION

The artist who shows the grizzly bear wounded on the Upper Missouri in 1832 should have become noted. It is a splendid scene. The hills in the distance, the perfect action of the hind-quarters of the bear slinking away, the pained expression on the face, and in the ears and eyes of the wounded animal. I wonder who the Mr. Bodmer was who did such work ninety-nine years ago?

So they killed two deer with bird shot in 1833! Looks to me like a long shot for number eight's and ten's. Killing a deer from a horse galloping at full speed in 1832 was a great feat, but I remember a story of a foxhunter who lived only three miles from here. He was driving a pair of horses hitched to a democrat wagon full gallop down the road. A friend of his was standing up behind drawing a bead on a fox they chased down the road for half a mile. When they got close to red rover the driver yelled, "Now, give it to him, Dave!" and Dave did and got him.

It is interesting to note that the East had become so civilized that the bow and arrow, once the chief weapon of America, had to be reintroduced in 1838 by the United Bowmen of Philadelphia.

A buffalo hunt, in 1840, is the real thing, but a little tough on the bull as there are six men to the one animal. I remember well when every horse-car driver in Worcester had his buffalo coat. They cost ten to fifteen dollars then and now it's harder to find a good buffalo skin than it is to locate a needle in a haystack.

Mention is made of Lady Suffolk, who trotted three miles in 7:32½ on the Beacon Course. The great mare was immortalized in Forester's *Horses in America* with an exquisite steel engraving by H. Clarke, showing the mare with braided mane, trotting with a fine stride, pricked ears, steadfast eyes and nostrils wide open, being ridden by a jockey holding a tight rein, seated in the saddle with a crupper around the tail, and beside the track on a stone is engraved "The Magic 2:26" and under that the year, 1843.

We find a picture of Ripton and Confidence in 1844 at Long Island, in high-wheeled sulkies. My, how snappy they look! The trotting match at Union Course, Long Island, back in 1851 will interest many. There's the same old familiar grand-stand under which the drivers met after each heat to decide who should win the next, and bet accordingly. Then in the judges' stand are the same type of judges who when a 2:40 horse trotted in :35 would hang out a :40 as they didn't want to hurt the owner's feelings.

Later we read about the great Flora Temple and opposite my steel engraving by Louis Maurer of this great bob-tail mare driven to sulky by Jim McMann I find a list of the trotting horses sketched and lithographed by that talented artist, from 1852-70, all written in his own handwriting. Down at the bottom is a note which states that, "steel engraving of Flora Temple and Highland Maid was the first racing picture I ever did for Currier & Ives."

INTRODUCTION

The two pictures of the Fashion Race Course are worth the price of the whole book. What a splendid grandstand, made of stone and one hundred yards long with the stars and stripes floating over the central portion. It would be well to send this to Matt Winn so that he might build a real grandstand at Churchill Downs, Kentucky, whose present stand is hardly better than one at a country fair; but the engineer in laying out the Fashion Course made four sharp turns all as bad as Tattenham Corner at Epsom Downs.

A delightful sketch of the Prince of Wales shooting chickens on the prairies is dated 1860. I remember how every year, long, long ago, the late Jerome Marble would start out from Worcester with his private Pullman car and a host of friends for the western prairies. He always came back with wonderful tales of their success and photographs of the car draped with antelope, deer, bears and chickens.

Two of Catlin's sketches are shown, one a buffalo hunt and the other flagging an antelope. Catlin not only lived with the buffalo in America, but with royalty in England for he introduced his party of nine Ojibway Indian braves and squaws in full war paint and feathers, with necklaces of bears' teeth, and belts about their waists ornamented with heads and masks of foxes and 'coons, to the Queen and Prince Consort at Windsor Castle. The party was served with a repast consisting principally of roast beef, washed down with champagne which they drank to the Queen's health.

Many a reader of these pages will remember when he followed the moose in the snow day after day in Maine or New Brunswick, praying for rain to form a crust which would hinder the moose and enable the hunter on snowshoes to run the animal down and get within shot of him.

Along the pages we find about Thomas Bangs Thorpe born in Westfield, not far from Worcester, and his picture in *The Bee Hunter* of a wild turkey gobbler is one of the best I have seen. Up in Petersham at My Shooting Box the oldest inhabitants used to tell of when wild turkeys were plentiful in the woods now making up the Harvard Forest, and as for wildcats, four were shot within two miles of my place there last winter.

How amusing the pictures of the Tenpin and Billiard Players! That of the Cricket Match in 1844 brings to my mind the games that were played in Worcester, as we had a Cricket team made up of the Englishmen working at the Whittall Carpet Mills.

The prize fight between Morrissey and Benecia Boy reminds me of the death of Squire Abingdon Baird of England, who brought Charlie Mitchell, prize fighter, to New York and later stood by the ringside when Jim Hall fought, one cold wet night in New Orleans. Norvin Harris, the well known southern sportsman told me at the Boston Club, New Orleans, that the Squire caught such a bad cold that night that within three days he died of pneumonia. The death of Squire Abingdon voided his

Derby nomination of the favorite, Meddler, and William H. Forbes who was searching through England for a stallion to head his Neponset stud near Milton, Massachusetts, bought the great stallion at half his value.

So ladies used to race on the fairgrounds at Housatonic Agricultural Society, Great Barrington, Massachusetts, 1857?

The ladies' races at Great Barrington were on the flat, and in 1930 Mrs. Geraldyn Redmond won the Diana Stakes on the flat in Aiken, and the race was carried off in 1931 by Miss Regan. In the fall of 1930 Mrs. Redmond also won the ladies' steeplechase at Essex, New Jersey and in the spring of 1931 Miss Jean Olcott won the Aiken Hunters Steeplechase, open to men and women, over twenty-five jumps on the Aiken drag line.

In the text I find the words, "Gentlemen of the city often played in the orchestra at the theatre." Yes, and my father and grandfather used to play the base viol and the violin and sing in the choir of the Barre church near Smithville where their mills were located; and no race meeting at The Country Club in olden days was considered a success unless, after the races, Billy Seabury, a member of the exclusive Somerset Club, with baton in hand led the brass band and then played many of the instruments.

Robert Bonner was the nationally known publisher of the New York *Ledger*. Mr. Bonner began driving for his own amusement and started a stable in 1856. After the war between the States he became the greatest supporter of strictly amateur driving. I have before me a letter from the office of the *Ledger* in Mr. Bonner's own handwriting, in answer to an attack upon his ownership of horses. It is dated, New York, July 30, 1872, Cor. Spruce & William Streets, and reads in part as follows:

"Private to the Editor of the Worcester Spy:

It is true I own good horses, but any man who states that I keep them for advertising my paper or myself is in a language of our 'later Franklin' a willful and malicious liar, not merely that, but in attributing such a sordid motive to me he shows that he himself is imbued with the instincts of low and ungenerous nature.

I own good horses because I *love* good horses and I think that a man *can* own good horses without making a gambler of himself. I do not think that the Almighty ever made anything for the use of man of which man is bound to use a mean specimen when he can honestly afford to use a good one. If he did why then all good men,— clergymen, editors — should be prohibited from using any horses except broken-down spavined and foundered nags.

Yours truly,

Robert Bonner."

The title, Westchester Polo Club at Jerome Park, 1876, brings to my memory that Frank Gray Griswold collected the money for the Westchester Cup which was won by the Englishmen at Newport and is now the international polo trophy; there is also a charming picture of the Queens County Hounds founded by Mr. Griswold and of which he was Master for many years.

The sketch 1867 shows how wild pigeons were murdered and we hear that at night they used to knock them off trees with sticks. I remember spending an afternoon trailing the last pair of wild pigeons known in the world, in Cincinnati and found them in the zoo. That was years ago.

Goldsmith Maid is a treasured memory in every sportsman's mind and there are some who will read this book who saw her beat American Girl in 1869, driven to a high sulky. The trotters surely had their day on Harlem Lane in 1870, and the horse next to the pair, shown in the picture of this, I am sure is Dexter with his white face and stockings.

Goldsmith Maid was at her best when I was a boy in 1874, and I carry indelibly stamped in my memory the fact that she never was started in a race until she was eight years old. Not being trained until she was fully developed, she was able to campaign year after year until her death from pneumonia at twenty. She won more races than any horse ever foaled, $362,000 in money at meetings for trotters, not runners, with one Futurity worth over $120,000. With this in mind I have always decried hard trials for young runners or trotters. Well do I remember the thrill that went through every horseman in the village of Worcester when "The Maid" trotted three heats at Boston in 2:16½, 2:15½, and 2:14¾, the latter the fastest record to that date.

Gray Parker surely drew a scream in his sketch of the beaux and belles at the Club House, Jerome Park, 1875. Looks like Lord Dundreary, Lily Langtry, "Beauty" Beech, Lillian Russell and others of stage and society fame.

When we see them playing polo on the lawn of the new polo club house, Jerome Park, 1876, and think of the fifteen or twenty fields now within twenty-five miles of Meadow Brook, Long Island, it shows that the world has moved on.

Again Gray Parker depicts the opening day at Jerome Park and the start for the Withers Stake, half of the riders going one way and the other half going the other way. Some money burned up!

Delancey Kane's coach in front of the Hotel Brunswick will be a fine memory to hundreds. Many of us have had our morning meal in the breakfast room that looked out on the avenue of that dear old hostelry when food was food and service was service.

Such a splendid page illustration, dated 1877,— the first annual bench show of the Westminster Kennel Club which the title of the sketch states was at the Hippodrome, the abandoned railroad station of the New York Central Railroad, also called Gilmore's Gardens. The sketch shows the grand trophy to the best setter, given by Tiffany and Company, and also a cut of the head of the pointer, Sensation, which for years adorned the catalogues and all the champion medals of the Westminster Kennel Club and is still their insignia.

Baseball is not my line, but I have before me *Casey at the Bat*, by Ernest Lawrence Thayer, who was a class-mate of my brother's and a great friend of mine. He wrote this baseball epic while on the San Francisco *Examiner* but was so modest about it that for years a number of others claimed the authorship. When De Wolf Hopper came to Worcester we advised him beforehand that Mr. Thayer, the author, would be at the theatre and the actor gave us a box. After the last act he came out on the stage and in a charming speech paid his respects to the author and told the audience of the wonderful value *Casey at the Bat* had been to his bank account.

How well I remember chasing in the morning for the Worcester *Spy* to find out whether Weston or Rowell was ahead in the long-distance Madison Square Garden contest.

Miss Elsa von Blumen on a high bicycle reminds me of the time I held the American record for a few months after riding a cone bearing, Standard Columbia, solid tire, non-ball-bearing pedals, high bicycle from Worcester to Boston and back, ninety miles, beginning at five in the morning and landing back home at eight that night, when I was only fifteen. Yes, I was tired that night. The Wheelmen in Boston brings me back to the parades in Springfield where we all used to ride to the bicycle races there each fall. How proudly we perched up on high, coasting with our legs over the handle bars, until we struck a washout in the dirt roads, (there were no others then), and a hard fall that followed promptly erased our proud moments.

The words about Lake Quinsigamond take me back to the boat races there years ago. The best location for sightseers where we used to drive in our carriage was at Regatta Point. At that time the bridge over the lake was a floating one and made of trunks of trees chained together with planks nailed across. This was followed by a causeway and later by the present grand cement bridge. The boat races at the lake started so much interest in Worcester that the Quinsigamond Boat Club was formed which is still in existence, and for many years it was the most difficult club in the Heart of the Commonwealth to join. I, like every youngster of course, was proud when I was elected. I can remember that for a few months I rowed a single scull but gave it up as it was a dreary sport always going over the same water.

The paragraphs about Ned Hanlon and Courtney will thrill many. As a boy I used to take swimming and rowing lessons at O'Leary's boat house where they kept their shells and I can see that perfectly proportioned Indian-tanned young Canadian carrying his shell down to the float now. It must have been 1883-5 when Hanlon and Courtney were at O'Leary's.

The reader of the passage on Captain Bogardus should appreciate that in the early days the original glass balls were filled with feathers so that when the ball was broken the feathers floated in the air.

The sentences telling of tennis at Newport will interest hundreds, for all New England used to journey down on the terrible trains to the annual tournaments there. So keen were we youngsters, (three of us Smiths had won the championship for Worcester County), that we started early in the morning and came back late at night, but saw Sears, Slocum, Campbell, Beeckman and others win their championships, and with bated breath we used to tell of the owls with glass eyes illuminated by gaslight which were on the gateposts of James Gordon Bennett's bachelor quarters just opposite the Casino.

As Tennyson has so beautifully said: "Memory — slipping back upon the golden days." Certainly we are grateful to our author, Herbert Manchester, who with unwearying eye has searched here, there, and everywhere, and selected from thousands of manuscripts, books, papers and periodicals of the past four hundred years these speaking pictures and illuminating facts which carry our minds back to our golden days.

Lordvale,
North Grafton, Mass.,
October 6th, 1931.

Harry Worcester Smith

"For the Sake of Sport in America."

FOUR CENTURIES OF
SPORT IN AMERICA

Aztecs hunting. From an Aztec manuscript

Aztec god killing a jaguar. From an Aztec miniature

FOUR CENTURIES OF AMERICAN SPORT

THE EARLIEST RECORDS

THE earliest records of sport in North America go back to the miniature paintings in the manuscripts of the Aztecs. While these Mexican hieroglyphics are still not entirely understood, among them may be discerned various groups representing, in a symbolic way, hunting, trapping, fishing, and related scenes. The miniatures are vivid with color, wonderfully decorative, and crowded with action.

Some depict the slaying of a jaguar by a god, others the killing of an ocelot, the snaring of a deer, the spearing of a shark, or the shooting of rabbits with bows and arrows.

How King Montezuma himself went hunting is narrated by Bernal Diaz del Castillo, an officer under Cortes during the conquest of Mexico. The Spaniards were building a sailboat, and, says Diaz, "When Montezuma heard of it, he said to Cortes that he wished to go hunting on a rocky island standing in the lake."

A highly interesting feature of this event was that the island "was preserved so that no one dared to hunt there, however great a chief he might be, under pain of death." Such a restriction would probably be unheard of in a wholly savage community, and indicates the semi-civilization of the Aztecs as well as the greatness of Montezuma.

No details are given of the king's hunting except that "he arrived at Penol, which was not far off, and Montezuma killed all the game he wanted, deer and hares and rabbits, and returned very contented to the city."

In the capital near his palace were an aviary, where all sorts of birds from his dominions were raised, and an aquarium, which was filled with many varieties of fish.

In the account of Montezuma's hunt, jaguars and panthers are not mentioned, no doubt because they were kept off the preserve for the protection of the other game. By what means the Mexicans hunted them is described by Acosta, in his *Natural and Moral History of the Indies*, written in Spanish in 1588.

Of the panther hunt he says: "The Indians assemble in troupes to hunt the mountain lion, and form, as it were, a circle, which they call chacu, wherewith they environ them, and afterward they kill them with stones, clubs, and other weapons. These lions are wont to climb trees where, being mounted high up, the Indians kill them with lances and crossbows, but more easily with harquebuses."

The jaguars were larger than the panthers and were long called tigers by the early writers. According to Acosta, "These tigers are more fierce and cruel and are more dangerous to meet, because they break forth and assail men treacherously. They are spotted as the historiographers describe them. I have heard some report that these tigers were very fierce against the Indians but would not adventure at all against the Spaniards, or very little, and that they would choose an Indian in the midst of many Spaniards and carry him away."

On occasions the hunt by men in a circle was enlarged to a general chase or round-up. A favorite place for this was the Zacatepes Forest near the capital. In the middle of this the hunters set snares and nets, and then thousands of beaters formed a circle of from six to eight miles. They set fire to the brush and raised a great din, before which the game fled to the center, where were the nets and snares. As the circle contracted, the hunters attacked the animals with arrows and lances. Many were killed and many taken, the total forming an immense number.

So great were the reports of the game slain in this way that the first viceroy sent from Spain refused to believe them, and ordered a special hunt of this sort repeated on the great plain in the country of the Otomies.

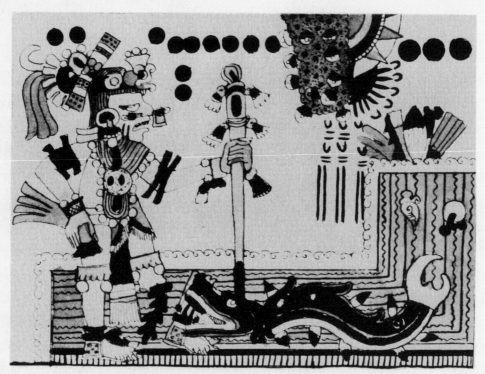

An Aztec killing a great fish. From an Aztec miniature

An Aztec conception of a Spanish horse.
From an Aztec miniature

[3]

So in the same way a circle was formed by over 11,000 beaters, and such a great quantity of game was driven together that the viceroy commanded nearly all of it to be set at liberty. Nevertheless, according to Toribio Motolinia, who wrote at the time, they killed over 600 deer, 100 coyotes, and a great quantity of lesser game. The place was long called the Cazadero or Place of the Chase.

Besides bows and arrows, spears, darts, nets, and snares, the Aztecs had blowpipes, which they used in killing small birds. In the case of the kings and chiefs, these tubes were ornamented with gold or silver, or engraved and painted.

They employed a unique stratagem in capturing ducks, which frequented the lakes in thousands. First they placed in the water empty gourds which the ducks would peck at and soon become accustomed to. Then the hunter would fit a gourd over his head and conceal the rest of his body beneath the water, and when a duck came to peck at the gourd, would seize it by the legs.

For catching fish they made use of harpoons, nets, and hooks, and so great was the abundance in the lakes that they had little difficulty supplying themselves.

In attacking alligators, skilled and daring hunters would sometimes take a short, stout pike or stake, sharpened on both ends, and, waiting for the alligator to come at them mouth open, would insert it by hand perpendicularly so far into the gaping mouth that the jaws could not close. After the alligator was thus rendered less dangerous, it was turned over and dispatched.

As is invariably the case in a savage or wild country, such sports were closely connected with the providing of food or clothing, but the Aztecs had a few recreations more nearly approaching games.

There were foot races, to which the Aztecs were trained from childhood, and sham battles, in which the warriors took part. More especially, there was a sort of foot ball, which was played with a ball of "elastic gum," — a term that no doubt signifies rubber.

The game was played between walls, which served as goals, by from one to three persons on a side. They were not allowed to touch the ball with their feet or hands, but only with their joints, such as the knee, hip, shoulder and elbow. In the middle of the court there were also two large stones with holes through them, and if a player should manage to drive the ball through one of these holes, it was accounted a miracle, and all the other players and spectators were expected to present him with their clothes.

This game must have been quite common because there were many such balls sent as tribute from the provinces to the capital.

The first horses seen by the Indians of the mainland of North America were those brought into Mexico by Cortes. When the Aztecs first saw them they took the horse and man to be one animal, — a mistake such as had no doubt given rise to the conception of the mythological centaur in prehistoric Greek times. At first the Aztecs worshipped the horse, considering it of the same godlike nature that they did the conquerors themselves.

A few of the Aztec miniatures in their manuscripts of that period give an idea of the horses introduced by the Spaniards, as seen by Aztec eyes. The most impressive of them depict a horse approximating the Barb which was introduced into Spain by the Moors. This was the type ridden by the men at arms. The animals ridden by the priests are pictured very differently. They were smaller and less rangy and, we suspect, in some cases the gentle burro.

The horse was taken northward by Coronado in his march in search of Quivara in 1541, where it made just as much impression upon the Indians as it had upon the Aztecs. In 1583, when Antonio de Espeho visited the Hopi Indians of Arizona, they also considered the animal divine, and spread cotton mantles on the ground for the horses to walk on.

How early some of the horses brought into the southwestern part of the present United States escaped and formed wild herds is uncertain, but it must have been some decades later, because the early descriptions of the

Florida Indians attacking an alligator. Le Moyne, 1564

Indians stalking deer. Le Moyne, 1564

[7]

Indians of the southern plains do not credit them with possessing horses.

The earliest pictures of hunting within the present boundaries of the United States are the drawings of Jacques Le Moyne, the artist who accompanied Laudonniere in the French expedition to Florida. Engravings were made from them and appeared in 1564 in his account of the expedition, and were duplicated in De Bry's *Florida* in 1590.

One of these engravings represents the Indian method of stalking deer under cover of a deerskin, and is explained by Le Moyne as follows:

"The Indians have a way of hunting deer which we never saw before. They manage to put on the skins of the largest which have previously been taken, in such a manner, with the heads on their own heads, that they can see out of the eyes as through a mask. Thus accoutred, they can approach close to the deer without frightening them. They take advantage of the time when the animals come to drink at the stream, and having their bows and arrows all ready, easily shoot them, as they are plentiful in those regions."

The Florida Indians, who were greatly harassed by alligators and had to keep a guard on watch against them, had evolved a method of slaying them that combined both safety and effectiveness. They put up near a river a little hut full of cracks and holes from which a watchman could see and hear the alligators a long way off. For according to Le Moyne, "When driven by hunger, they come out of the rivers and crawl about on the islands after prey, and if they find none, they make such a frightful noise that it can be heard for half a mile."

The watcher thereupon called the rest of the hunters, who were lying in readiness, and taking a ten- or twelve-foot pole from the trunk of a young tree, they set forth after the monster. When "they come up with him," says Le Moyne, as "he is crawling along with his mouth wide open, all ready to catch one of them if he can, with the greatest quickness they punch the pole, small end first, as deep as possible down his throat, so that the roughness and irregularity of the bark may hold it from being got out again."

When the monster was thus disabled, since its back was so protected by scales as to be almost impenetrable to their weapons, they turned it on its back and pierced its belly, which was softer, with pikes.

Another engraving in Le Moyne illustrates Indians fishing from a pirogue, which was made from half of a tree trunk by hollowing it out with stone hatchets and fire.

In De Bry's *Virginia*, 1590, in the background of the portrait of an Indian, appear faint details of Indians in a canoe shooting at ducks with a bow and arrow, and Indians on foot armed with the same weapon and chasing a deer.

THE SEVENTEENTH CENTURY

Sports of the Indians

In the seventeenth century, when the French began to explore the St. Lawrence, the Great Lakes, and the Mississippi, the accounts of Indian sports began to penetrate farther inland.

In his narrative of his voyages and discoveries between 1615 and 1618, Samuel de Champlain describes an elaborate deer drive which was staged for his entertainment and in which he himself took part.

After a journey of several days, his force came to a forest of firs, where the Indians constructed a palisade of great stakes of wood closely pressed together and eight or nine feet high. The palisade was in the form of a triangle open on one side and with the other sides some fifteen hundred paces long. At the point of the triangle was a small opening only five feet wide which led into a little enclosure, also in the shape of a triangle, which was covered in part with boughs.

The Indians were so rapid at this construction that they completed the enclosure in less than ten days, during which time other Indians supplied the needs of the company by catching trout and pike of prodigious size.

After all preparations were made, the Indians set out an hour before daybreak, and about half a league from the opening of the enclosure, formed a long line, with an Indian every eighty paces or so. Each had two sticks which he struck together to make a racket, and thus they marched slowly toward the opening of the angle.

The deer, frightened by the noise, fled before them and were driven into the wide mouth of the palisades. The hunters, drawing closely together as they reached the palisades, forced the deer along the inner sides, and as they approached the point of the enclosure, began to shout and imitate the yelping of wolves, which were natural foes of the deer. The deer, frightened by the din, crowded through the little opening into the small enclosure, which was so strong that they could not escape. There they were easily dispatched by arrows and lances.

"I assure you," remarked Champlain, "there is a singular enjoyment in this chase, which took place every two days, and was so successful that in the thirty-eight days during which we were there, they captured 120 deer, which they made good use of, reserving the fat, which they use as we do butter, for winter, and taking to their homes part of the flesh for their feasts."

Champlain calls attention to the snares which the Indians set to capture deer, and illustrates one in his engraving.

The skins were worked up for clothing, the Indians tawing (this is a different process from tanning) them with brains until they resembled chamois.

One has the feeling, in reading Champlain's account of this drive, that it was rather a great sporting event given for his delectation and entered into with élan by the Indian braves, than a mere pot hunting expedition. The younger Indians hunted not only from necessity but for sport and the honors and ornaments that came from a successful chase.

Sports of the Colonists

Probably the first picture of the sports of the American colonists is an engraving in a section of De Bry, published in 1619 and giving an account of Virginia. The engraving illustrates a passage in a Latin translation of Captain John Smith's *Description of New England*, printed in 1619. It shows one planter on a horse and accompanied by a dog, chasing a stag; another fishing, and still another with a gun on his shoulder for fowling. Most astonishing of all, several planters are engaged in falconry, two

Equestris ordinis viri , quibus exercitiis sese in Virginia oblectari possint.

Quest ris ordinis viri variis exercitiis ludicris animum possunt recreare. Indies enim datur occasio loca incognita, silvasque remotas venatus piscatus atque aucupii gratia adeundi; ubi diversi generis feræ variique fructus non sine voluptate sese offerunt. Videas in amœnis portubus, sex septem aut octo accipitres ex alto præcipites ferri, ac duas circiter horas piscium capitibus advolutos, suum inde pabulum quærere. Alibi videbis illos reliquas aves persequi, adunco vostro contundere, atque in terram prosternere: quæ res lepidum intuentibus præbet spectaculum. Ipsi vero accipitres, utut feri sint, facili negotio cicurari possunt.

Recreations of Gentlemen in Virginia, 1619

carrying hawks on their wrists while another is reaching for the quarry.

This brings up the question as to whether falconry was ever indulged in by the colonists. As a matter of fact this feature of the illustration is not justified by the passage in Smith's description, which runs as follows:

"For gentlemen, what exercise should more delight them than ranging daily those unknowne parts, using fowling and fishing for hunting and hawking? And yet you shall see the wilde hawkes give you some pleasure, in seeing them stoope (six or seven after one another) an houre or two together, at the skule of fish in the faire harbours, as those a-shore at foule; and never trouble nor torment yourselves with watching, mewing, feeding, and attending them: nor kill horse and man with running and crying, 'See you a hawk?'

"For hunting also; the woods, lakes, and rivers afford not only chace sufficient, for any that delights in that kind of toyle or pleasure; but such beasts to hunt, that besides the delicacy of their bodies for food, their skins are so rich, as may well recompense the dayly labour with a captain's pay."

This account is surely an argument against, rather than for, falconry at that date in Virginia, yet there are, later, a few scattered notices indicating the occasional employment of hawks.

The oldest notices of games among the colonists are mostly prohibitions against them at certain times or in places where they were thought liable to foment gambling or discord. In 1647 in Massachusetts Bay, for example, we have a court order against shuffleboard in the following terms:

"Upon complaynt made of great disorder that hath bin observed and is lik to increase, by the use of the game called shovelboard, it is therefore ordered and enacted by the authoritie of this Court, that no person shall henceforth use the said game of shoffleboard in any house of common entertaynment."

In 1650 this prohibition was extended against "bowling or any other play or game in or about howses of common entertaynment."

In contrast with such games, however, archery was considered a safe-guard against failure of ammunition, and in 1647 Rhode Island ordered that every father provide each male child between seven and seventeen years of age with a bow and two arrows, and that every person between seventeen and seventy have a bow and four arrows.

Interdictions were not confined to New England. Racing within the city limits of New Amsterdam was prohibited in 1657. Then we find Governor Pieter Stuyvesant proclaiming a day of fast in 1659 providing:

"We shall interdict and forbid, during divine service on the day afore-said, all exercise and games of tennis, ball-playing, hunting, fishing, plowing and sowing, and moreover all unlawful practices such as dice, drunkenness — "

The notice of tennis in this provision is especially interesting as evidence that court tennis must have been played in the city while it was still in possession of the Dutch. The ball playing mentioned, no doubt included bowling, which was a favorite game with the Dutch.

Governor Stuyvesant's order was merely temporary, and it should be added that New Amsterdam never had any set of prohibitions to compare with those by the New England colonies.

In the winter, sleighing and skating were popular, and possibly some of the Dutch games on ice were introduced.

The great hunting place near New York was Long Island. In 1670 Daniel Denton enumerated the game there as follows:

"For Wilde Beasts, there is Deer, Bear, Wolves, Foxes, Racoon, Otters, Musquashes, and Skunks. Wild Fowl there is great store of, as Turkies, Heath-Hen, Quailes, Partridges, Pigeon, Cranes, Geese of several sorts, Brants, Ducks, Widgeon, Teal, and divers others."

Probably the first instance of the encouragement of racing by the government of a colony was by Governor Nicholls in New York in 1665. In 1669 racing was reëstablished on a more permanent footing by an order of Governor Lovelace. His letter is addressed to the "Justices of the Peace, constable, and overseers of Hempstead concerning the Horse Race," and begins, "Col. Nicholls, my worthy Predecessor, having beene pleased the Last yeare, to Constitute a horse Race in Your partes, not so much for the divertisement of the Youth alone but for the Encouragement of the bettering the breed of horses which through great neglect is so Impaired that they afford very inconsiderable Rates:

"Being therefore willing to advance any designe that shall tend to a Publique good, I have thought to advertise you that I appoint the race shall be Runne on the   of May next ensuing."

The governor goes on and arranges the details of the meeting as follows:

" I shall desire of you that you'll take the subscriptions of all such in your partes as are disposed to Run for a Crowne in sylver or the value in good wheate, and you are likewise to send the List of the last yeares subscribers to Capt. Salisbury, who I have appointed to receive them. I hope, having this tymely notice, you will cause such provision to be made for Receipt of men and horses (for their money) that they may be accommodated like loving friends and neighbors. I am

Fort James,   Your friend,
April 1st, 1669.   Frank Lovelace."

The next year Daniel Denton wrote that the best horses on the island were brought there to try their swiftness, and the winner rewarded with a silver cup, two being provided for that purpose.

This track on Hempstead Plain was later called New Market Course, after the famous one in England, and was in occasional use for many decades.

In contrast with this policy, Plymouth Colony in 1674 enacted through the court, that whatsoever person ran a race with any horse in any street or common road should forfeit five shillings or sit in the stocks for one hour. This was not, however, a prohibition against racing off the public thoroughfares.

The greatest center of horse racing in the colonies in the seventeenth century was no doubt Virginia, though the chief evidences for it are the many disputes over the payment of wagers which reached the court records.

One of the first of these records is not only unique as an anecdote of sport but throws a significant spotlight upon Virginia society of that day.

In 1673 James Bullock, a tailor of York County, ran his mare against a horse of Matthew Slader for 2,000 pounds of tobacco and won the race; but the bet was not paid, and he took it into court. There he not only could not collect the wager, but was fined one hundred pounds of tobacco by the court, which decided that it was contrary to law for him to race, declaring "racing to be a sport for gentlemen only."

The next year appear records of Smith's Field, where races were run in Northampton County, and soon afterward of the Coan Race Course, which long continued to be used as a center in Westmoreland County.

At Devil's Field in Surrey County in 1678 the two judges disagreed. The same year at Bermuda Hundred in Henrico County the horses were ridden by servants, though usually the young bloods had handled their own. In the same county, the race course at Varina was highly spoken of in 1687 and continued to be popular for decades.

From Virginia, racing spread into Maryland, which was closely associated with the older colony, and became almost as much a feature of social life there as south of the Potomac.

The shores of the Chesapeake offered suitable ground for foxhunting, and there are a few Maryland notices of this sport as early as the middle of the seventeenth century, though it was not formal as in England, and each planter supplied a few hounds.

The best early source of data for several sorts of hunting in America is Baron de Lahontan, who travelled here between 1683 and 1694. Besides corroborating Champlain's account of a deer drive, he describes several hunts in which he took part. He writes in 1686 of how his party would find the tracks of elk in the snow and follow them for a league or two until they came upon herds of from five to twenty. The elk would take to flight through the snow, which was at times up to their breast. When the snow was soft the chase lasted for four or five leagues, but when it was hard or crusted over, they might come up with the elk in a quarter of a league. Sometimes, also, the dogs would stop them when the snow was very deep.

But at all events, when the elk were caught, it was not difficult to dispatch them, because they floundered somewhat in the snow. This was the same method of hunting elk in winter that was afterward adopted by the colonists.

In a letter of May, 1687, Lahontan describes how the Indians in duck hunting built floating huts holding four or five men and covered over with branches. Around these they placed decoys made of the skins of geese, ducks, and bustards, dried and stuffed with hay. When the waterfowl, which frequented the lake in infinite numbers and variety, saw the decoys, they would approach near the blinds and give the hunters a chance to shoot them either in the water or while flying. Then the Indians would get into their canoes and pick them up.

This account of the use of decoys by the Indians is remarkable both as an evidence of their inventiveness, and as a date in the history of decoys.

The same device was adopted by the colonists and became probably the most favored method of hunting waterfowl. Moreover, it should be noted how many of the devices employed by the Indians in hunting were imitated by the whites. Certainly the colonists in general learned more of hunting from the Indians than the knowledge of it which they brought with them from Europe. To the Indian's stratagems and woodcraft, they added the efficiency of the flintlock, the effect of which was to reduce the skill required.

Lahontan's account of wild pigeon shooting begins with a reference to a curious old church custom: "Then we resolved to carry on war against the pigeons, which are so numerous in Canada that the Bishop has been forced to excommunicate them more than once, because of the damage they do to the products of the earth."

He writes that they found the trees covered with pigeons outnumber-

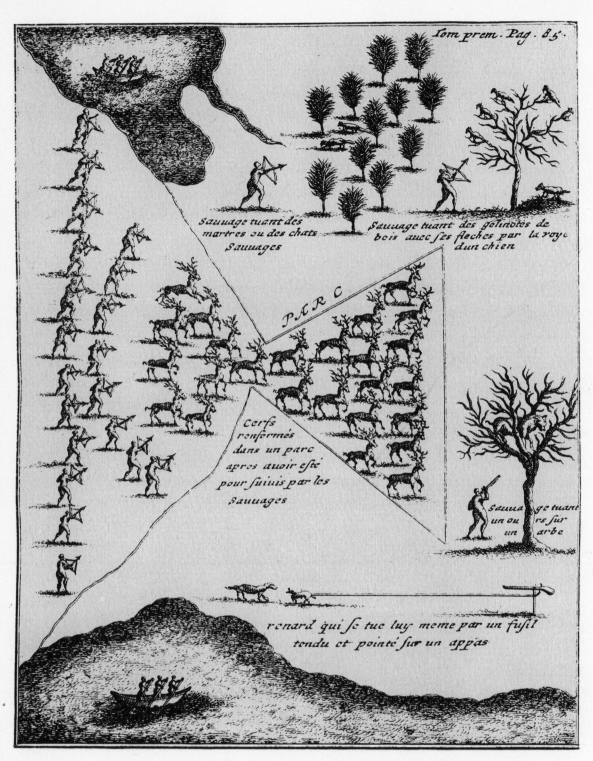

Sauuage tuant des
martres ou des chats
Sauuages

Sauuage tuant des golinotes de
bois auec ses fleches par la voye
dun chien

PARC

Cerfs
renfermés
dans un parc
apres auoir esté
pour suiuis par les
Sauuages

Sauua ge tuant
un ou rs sur
un arbe

renard qui se tue luy meme par un fusil
tendu et pointé sur un appas

*A deer drive; shooting martens; hunting wood hens with the aid of a dog;
shooting a bear, and a fox trap, 1683-1694*

ing the leaves, for it was the season when they were collecting to migrate south, and one would have thought that all the pigeons on earth had chosen to pass through that place. During the eighteen or twenty days his party stayed there he declares, "I firmly believe that a thousand men might have fed upon them heartily without any difficulty."

A few days later his party went bear hunting, and Lahontan marvelled at the skill of the savages in singling out the trees in which a bear was hidden. "When I heard one savage call to another, as we were walking up and down in a forest at a hundred paces from one another, 'Here's a bear,' I asked him how he knew there was a bear up in the tree that he knocked with his ax, and they all replied that it was as easily noted as the track of an elk's foot in the snow."

Five or six times in succession, when the savages had found such a tree, they knocked two or three times on the trunk with the ax, and the bear came out and was shot.

The white men later learned this method of bear hunting, and there are subsequent accounts of bear hunting by the pioneers which reproduce this description in detail. Lahontan wrote that the most curious thing he saw was the stupidity of the woodhens, which would sit upon the trees in flocks and be killed one after another without offering to stir. A very interesting detail is the way he says a dog would mark the tree they were on: "I have plied this sort of fowling in the vicinity of our camps or habitations in the winter time with the help of a dog which found the trees by scent and then barked; upon which I approached the tree and found the fowls upon the branches."

Here we have an unexpected record of a sporting dog among the Indians, — of a dog that would locate woodhens on a tree, probably by both scent and sight, and announce the fact to the hunter by barking. Is it possible that the Indian dog had such almost never-mentioned uses, and was not a mere hanger-on which barked at every unusual noise or sight?

When the French in their exploration of the interior made their way up the Mississippi, they came upon the buffalo. Outside of vague mention, the earliest description of an American buffalo or bison hunt, which is also embellished with an engraving of the animal, is probably that of Louis Hennepin, 1693, in his account of Louisiana. When the savages discovered a large number of buffaloes together they assembled their whole tribe to surround the bulls. Then they set on fire the dry grass in a circle about them, leaving a few openings in the fire where they lay in ambush. When the buffaloes saw the advancing flames, they fled through the openings, where they were attacked by the savages, who by this stratagem sometimes killed six score in a day.

Something of this same method of surrounding a herd of buffaloes was delineated over half a century later by Le Page du Pratz, though he does not mention the use of fire.

In both descriptions the hunting was done on foot, and there is no intimation in the accounts or engravings of the employment of horses in the chase.

Indians hunting buffalo, 1758

[26]

THE EIGHTEENTH CENTURY

By the eighteenth century, the Puritan prejudice against games and sports had begun to subside, and we begin to find records of their public tolerance in Massachusetts.

In the *Boston News-Letter*, which was founded in 1704 and was the first American newspaper, there is an advertisement of 1714 that "the Bowling Green, formerly belonging to Mr. James Ivers in Cambridge-Street Boston, does now belong to Mr. Daniel Stevens at the British Coffee House in Queen-Street, . . . where all Gentlemen, Merchants, and others that have a mind to Recreate themselves shall be well accommodated."

In 1715 we find a notice that at Cambridge a "Twenty Pound Plate" will be run for, open to any "Horse, Mare, or Gelding, not exceeding 14½ hands high, carrying — stone weight," the entrance fee being twenty shillings.

Two years later the owners gave notice to the public that there would be a special race between two horses on Rumlymash Beach for ten pounds, and nothing was said about an admission charge.

On training days, wrote Madam Knight in 1704, the youth near New Haven diverted themselves by shooting at a target, the winner receiving some yards of red ribbon, which was tied around his hat with the ends streaming down his back.

The greatest of the aboriginal American games, lacrosse, was described in a memoir to M. de Vaudreuil of the French government in 1718. The Indians near Detroit played it much in the summer, using "a sort of little racket" and a "ball of wood somewhat larger than the balls used in tennis." They played naked except for breechclouts and moccasins, but painted their bodies all over. Twenty or more played on a side, starting the game at the center, and whichever reached the goal won. They often played village against village, the Poux against the Outsouacs or the Hurons, and laid heavy stakes.

Frenchmen had already begun to take part in the game with them, which was probably the beginning of its adoption by the whites.

In a like account, Pierre de Charlevoix in 1721 stated that the distance between the goals was sometimes half a league.

There was a similar game, but played without bats, in which the players on each side sought to throw the ball from hand to hand until there was a chance to hurl it over the goal.

Such great games, tribal and inter-tribal, indicate a love for sport among the braves, which helps to illuminate the spirit in which they entered upon their hunting. They sought excitement in the games, just as they enjoyed the excitement in the hunt.

In the South, the first details of various sorts of hunting are given by Robert Beverly, in his *History and Present State of Virginia*, published in 1705.

The Virginians had taught their horses to aid in stalking deer by walking gently by the hunter's side to cover him from the sight of the quarry. This reminds one of the previous Indian method of stalking by being concealed in a deerskin.

They hunted rabbits with swift, mongrel dogs, which either caught them or forced them to seek a hollow tree, whence they were smoked out, unconscious but alive.

Raccoons and opossums were hunted afoot with small dogs by the light of the moon. When they were treed, a nimble fellow was sent up the tree to shake the beast off the end of the limb, which was usually accomplished after a scuffle, while the dogs kept up an excited yapping below.

Traps were set for wolves. Turkeys were both shot and trapped, and

Beverly adds, "A Friend of mine invented a great Trap, wherein he at times caught many Turkeys, and particularly seventeen at one time, but he could not contrive it to let others in after he had trapped the first flock."

The young men chased the horses that had grown up wild in the woods, but they were becoming very fast and so difficult to catch that frequently only aged ones or young colts could be taken.

Riding was not only the chief method of journeying, but, according to Hugh Jones in 1724, "The common Planters, leading easy Lives, don't very much admire Labour, or any manly Exercise, except Horse-Racing."

Nor did they have much of any diversion, if we believe Jones, except cock fighting, in which some greatly delighted.

In Maryland there is a record of 1730 that Mr. Smith, one of the foxhunting planters who were not satisfied with the sport they were getting from the chase of the grey fox, imported a number of English red foxes and after a dinner to celebrate the event set them at liberty along the Chesapeake. Many sportsmen have considered this the origin of the red fox in the eastern United States, but there are practically decisive evidences against it.

To begin with, Pehr Kalm, the Swedish naturalist, wrote in Philadelphia in 1748, "There are two species of foxes in the English colonies, the one grey and the other red." From this it is evident that the red fox was known at that date in other colonies besides Maryland, though Kalm says they were "very scarce here."

Kalm was assured by Mr. Bartram, the traveller and botanist, that "according to the unanimous testimony of the Indians this kind of foxes was never found in this country before the Europeans settled in it."

But he heard two different versions of how they came here. Mr. Evans, who made the journey with Mr. Bartram and Mr. Weiser to the Iroquois, told him of a popular tradition that, early in the settlement of the colonies, "a gentleman of fortune in New England who had a great inclination for fox hunting brought over a great number of foxes from Europe and let them loose in his territories that he might be able to indulge his passion for hunting." This could hardly be identified with the Maryland importation which was only eighteen years previous.

Mr. Bartram and several others had been told by the Indians that "these foxes came into America soon after the arrival of the Europeans, after an extraordinarily cold winter, when all the water to the northward was frozen."

This might point to an invasion from Canada across the Niagara or Lake Ontario. Certainly the red fox was known along the Great Lakes before 1730, because it was noted by Pierre de Charlevoix in his *Journal of a Voyage to North America*, undertaken by order of the French king. In this journey, he travelled all around the Great Lakes, and then down the Mississippi to New Orleans, and as the French were fur dealers he had many opportunities to examine pelts.

In 1721, in his seventh letter, Charlevoix described the different sorts of foxes in America as follows: "The fur of a certain species of black foxes, which live in the northern mountains, is still more esteemed. . . . They are, moreover, exceedingly rare, probably on account of the difficulty of catching them. There is a more common sort, the hair of which is black or grey, mixed with white; others of them are quite grey, and others again of a tawny red. Certain foxes are found in the Upper Mississippi Valley of infinite beauty, with fur of an argentine or silver grey."

Thus it looks as if the red fox were indigenous in Canada or the northern part of the United States, and gradually spread southward.

Whatever its source, in 1748 Kalm wrote that it was considered more noxious than the grey fox because it killed lambs, and that in Pennsylvania and other colonies there was a bounty for killing it. The pelt sold for two shillings and sixpence in Pennsylvania currency.

In the first part of the eighteenth century the notices of sports in New York became more varied. A notice of 1702 sets a value of £3 on an old billiard table. In 1704 Madame Knight tells of the great number of pleasure sleighs which went three or four miles out of town where they had houses of entertainment at a place called the Bowery.

At the right is Colonel Morris's yacht Fancy, 1719

View of Passaic Falls, 1766

[31]

The deer on Long Island and in Westchester had been hunted so much that they were rapidly decreasing in numbers, and in 1706 a closed season was established for their protection. Various private preserves were also enclosed, such as those of Governor Crosby and John Schuyler. In 1708 the closed season from April 1st to July 31st covered turkeys, heath hens, partridges and quails in Kings, Queens, and Suffolk counties.

In the large view of New York by Burgis, which was engraved about 1719, there is to be seen a small sloop, which according to the description below is "Collonel Morris's Fancy turning to Windward with a Sloop of Common Mould." This is in all likelihood the first engraving of an American yacht.

But there are other references to pleasure boats, which were sometimes barges. In 1732 Governor Montgomerie's "fine, large barge, with awnings and damask curtains" was to be sold at auction, as was Captain Rickett's Pleasure Boat (very well fitted) in 1736. Some years later the "Yacht or Pleasure Boat of Capt. Roddam" was for sale at Ackland's Coffee House.

In Philadelphia the Schuylkill Fishing Company was founded in 1732 as a club for anglers, and remains to-day as the oldest sporting or social club in the world.

It may surprise golfers, who think that the development of the game in America has taken place in the past generation, to learn that in 1729 the inventory of Governor Burnet of New York included "nine gouff clubs, one iron ditto, and seven dozen balls."

Bowling Green, at the beginning of Broadway, dates from 1732, when the city leased "a piece of land lying at the lower end of Broadway, fronting to the Fort," to John Chambers, Peter Bayard, and Peter Jay, all well known citizens, "to make a Bowling-Green thereof."

In order to check gambling, innkeepers in 1742 were forbidden to keep billiard tables, truck tables, or shuffle boards.

In 1721 the race over the Newmarket Course on Long Island was won by Samuel Bayard's horse. A notice appeared in 1736 that a race would be run on the "Course at New York" for a £20 plate, open to any carrying 10 stone and paying a pistole to enter. There was no admission for spectators on foot but a sixpence charge for those on horseback or in chaises. In 1742 there was a race on the Trinity Church Farms, west of what is now City Hall Park.

Foxhunting was introduced by the British officers, and was permitted in Flatbush after the fields were reaped, but was rather closely confined to the garrison.

Washington is reported to have hunted foxes in Virginia with Lord Fairfax, and the incident is illustrated in a later drawing by F. O. C. Darley.

Washington's foxhunting before the Revolution is thus described by his adopted son, G. W. Parke Custis:

"We have neither knowledge nor tradition of his having ever been a shooter or a fisherman: fox-hunting, being of a bold and animating character, suited well to the temperament of the 'lusty prime' of his age, and peculiarly well accorded with his fondness and predisposition for equestrian exercises.

"His kennel was situated about a hundred yards south of the family vault . . . . The building was of a rude structure but afforded comfortable quarters for the hounds; with a large enclosure paled in, having in the midst a spring of running water. The pack was very numerous and select, the colonel visiting and inspecting his kennel morning and evening, after the same manner as he did his stables. It was his pride (and a proof of his skill in hunting) to have his pack so critically drafted, as to speed and bottom, that in running, if one leading dog should lose the scent, another was at hand immediately to recover it, and thus when in full cry, to use a racing phrase, you might cover the pack with a blanket.

"During the season Mt. Vernon had many sporting guests from the neighborhood, from Maryland and elsewhere. Their visits were not of days but of weeks; and they were entertained in the good old style of Virginia's ancient hospitality. Washington, always superbly mounted in true sporting costume of blue coat, scarlet waistcoat, buckskin breeches,

Washington and Fairfax foxhunting

top boots, velvet cap, and whip with long thong, took the field at day-break with his huntsman, Will Lee, his friends and neighbors; and none more gallantly in the chase, nor with voice more cheerily awakened echo in the woodland, than he. . . . Such was the hunting establishment at Mount Vernon prior to the Revolution."

By the middle of the eighteenth century racing had developed to a sport of widespread importance.

About 1750 Colonel Tasker of Belair, Maryland, imported Selima, the daughter of the Godolphin Arabian. In 1752 she defeated Colonel Bird's Trial or Tryall, after an open challenge. Selima was the dam of Selim and others, with which Colonel Tasker was so successful that for some years Maryland-bred horses were barred from the Virginia Jockey Club purses. Thereupon Colonel Tasker sent his mares to Virginia to foal and in a few years was renewing his successes. In 1764 many of Colonel Tasker's horses, including several descendants of Selima, were sold at auction, but Selim continued his successes by beating True Briton in 1765 and 1766.

Under Governor Robert Eden, 1765-1775, Maryland racing entered upon its greatest period of fashion and popularity, and the course at Annapolis was probably the best in the country.

In 1750 a big race on Hempstead Plains, according to the *New York Postboy*, occasioned the transfer of more than seventy chairs and chaises over Brooklyn Ferry, and the presence of perhaps a thousand horses.

The best stables at that date in New York were kept by Oliver and James De Lancey and Lewis Morris. In 1754 one of Oliver De Lancey's horses made the round trip to Kingsbridge, twenty-eight miles, with one rider in an hour and forty-six minutes. James De Lancey's horse, True Briton, would take a five-barred gate time after time. A race around Beaver Pond in Jamaica in 1757 was won by Morris' horse, American Childers, which was famous at the time.

In 1764 James De Lancey's bay horse, Lath, won the Marconi Club's purse of £300, and five years later triumphed in a race at Philadelphia.

The English horse, Figure, in 1768 defeated the colonial-bred Salem, much to the chagrin of local breeders.

A record from Ipswich, Massachusetts, states that whereas horses had previously been taught by hobbles to pace, about 1770 they began to be allowed to trot.

The riding horses of Pennsylvania were characterized by Israel Acrelius in 1759 as real ponies, seldom over sixteen hands high! The country abounded in fast horses so that races were often made for very high stakes. A good riding horse would go more than a Swedish mile (about seven English miles) in an hour, and was not to be bought for less than six hundred dollars copper or one-tenth that in silver. It was thought that these horses had evolved from the wild horses from Virginia that had made their way northward.

The Reverend Andrew Burnaby wrote that in 1760 the gentlemen of Virginia, who were exceedingly fond of horse racing, had spared no trouble or expense to improve the breed by importing great numbers from England.

The first regularly organized foxhunting association in the United States was the Gloucester Fox Hunting Club, which was founded in Philadelphia in 1766, but did most of its hunting across the Delaware in Gloucester County, New Jersey.

One of the few records of falconry in America is a communication to the *Sporting Magazine*, England, that a large hawk shot in Yorkshire, England, had on one leg a brass band with the inscription, "Belonging to the Governor of New Halifax, America, A. D. 1762." It was shot in 1798 by the correspondent of the magazine.

THE REVOLUTIONARY ERA

An idea of the games in vogue in New York in pre-Revolutionary years is given in an advertisement of James Rivington in 1766, which states that he imported battledores and shuttlecocks, cricket balls, pellets,

Earliest American hunting print

best racquets for tennis and fives, and backgammon tables with men, boxes, and dice. Cocks for fighting were supplied to fanciers at the gentlemen's Coffee House. Bull baiting was advertised to take place on Tower Hill, every Thursday at 3 p.m. during the season of 1774.

The first known hunting scene actually engraved and published in the colonies, headed a piece of music in the *Royal American Magazine* of Boston in 1774. The words are as good as those of the average song, and, while no great poetry, have a certain ring:

THE HILL TOPS, A NEW HUNTING SONG

Now the Hill tops are Burnished with azure and gold,
And the prospect around us most bright to behold,
The Hounds are all trying the mazes to trace,
The Steeds are all neighing and pant for the Chace.

CHORUS

Then rouse each true Sportsman and join at the Dawn
The Song of the Hunterr, the Sound of the Horn,
The Sound of the Horn
The Song of the Hunterr, and the Sound of the Horn.

Health braces the Nerves and gives joy to the Face,
Whilst over the Heath we pursue the fleet Chace.
See the Downs now we leave and the Coverts appear,
As eager we follow the Fox or the Hare.

Where ever we go, pleasure waits on us still,
If we sink in the Valley, we rise on the Hill,
O'er Hedges and Rivers we valiantly fly,
Fearless of Death, we ne'er think we shall die.

From Ages long past by the Poets we're told
That Hunting was loved by the Sages of Old:
That the Soldier and Huntsman were both on a par,
And the Health giving Chace made them bold in the War.

When the Chace is once over, away to the Bowl,
The full flowing Bumper shall cheer up the Soul,
Whilst jocund our songs shall with Choruses ring,
And toasts to our Lasses, our Country and King.

Although the deer is not mentioned in the words, the engraving at the top depicts the death of the stag, and we suspect that in the last line of the second stanza, the poet originally wrote "deer" to rhyme with "appear" in the line above. The song, if it remained popular very long, must have been altered to blot out any reference to the king in the last line, for during the Revolution, already impending, street names were changed from royal titles and personages to more republican designations.

In that same year (1774) in Boston, Lord Percy built a yacht with a center board in order to demonstrate the advantage of that device. This was said to have worked satisfactorily, but due to the war coming on was not developed further at that time.

The greatest tragedy connected with lacrosse was in the conspiracy of Pontiac in 1763. The English had captured Quebec only four years before, but had alienated the Indians by their treatment of them. Pontiac, chief of the Ottawas, thereupon formed a conspiracy of many tribes against them and suddenly struck at the forts and settlements all along the Great Lakes. He induced the Ojibways to attack Fort Michillimackinac, but they did it by strategy. Either at Pontiac's suggestion or of their own devising, they staged a great game of lacrosse in honor of King George's birthday, June 4, 1763, between themselves and the Sacs on the great plain in front of the fort. There were hundreds, perhaps a thousand, on a side, naked except a loin-cloth and moccasins. The ball was tossed up between the two nations and the game began. The gates of the fort were open to permit the garrison better to see the sport, which became more and more exciting, while the ball, and the rushing, yelling masses of players came nearer and nearer the fort. When they came within a few rods, the game suddenly stopped, the players threw down their bats, drew their toma-hawks from their loin-cloths and charged through the open gates of the fort. The garrison were all killed or captured, and about the only ones who escaped death were a few whom the Ottawas demanded because they were not let into the battle.

A description of lacrosse as played by the Cherokee Indians in Florida was given by James Adair in 1775. The ball was made with deerskin stuffed hard with deer's hair. The bats were two feet long, with the lower end resembling the palm, but worked with deerskin thongs. The two parties were equal in number, and played for high stakes. The ball was put into play between the two goals and often kept in the air without touching the ground for a long time. A few valuable accounts of sports come from the midst of the Revolution. The Marquis of Chastellux, who travelled in America between 1770 and 1782, wrote that he happened upon a cockmain in Virginia to which planters had come from thirty miles.

A letter of Thomas Anbury, who states that he was an officer under General Burgoyne and sent with the captured army to the South, describes the sprint races near Charlottesville, Virginia, in 1779:

"I went with several officers to see a diversion peculiar to this country termed quarter-racing, which is a match between two horses to run a quarter of a mile in a straight direction, and near most of the ordinaries there is a piece of ground cleared in the woods for that purpose where there are two paths about six or eight yards assunder, which the horses run in. This diversion is a great favorite of the middling and lower classes, and they have a breed of horses to perform it with astonishing velocity, beating every other for that distance with the greatest ease." He writes that if one turned away his head the race was over before he saw it.

Anbury carefully distinguishes between these sprints and the long races in favor in the cities:

"These races are only among the settlers in the interior parts of this Province, for they are much laughed at and ridiculed by the people in the lower parts, about Richmond and other great towns: at Williamsburg is a very excellent course for two, three, or four-mile heats, where there are races every Spring and Fall; they run for purses generally raised by subscription, and the horse that wins two four-mile heats out of three is entitled to the prize, which is one hundred pounds the first day's running and fifty pounds every other day, and these races commonly last a week; at which very capital horses are started that would make no contemptible figure at Newmarket."

Diomed, the horse that won the English Derby in 1780, was in 1797 imported by Colonel John Hoomes of Virginia, to improve the breed there, and became the ancestor of a famous family of champions.

The first sporting book published in America was *The Sportsman's Companion*, apparently by a member of the British Army in New York. It was printed there in 1783, the year the British evacuated the city.

It treats of dogs and their training; of guns, powder, and shot; of grouse, partridges, and quail; of shooting parties; of improsperous days for hunting; of woodcocks and snipe; against intimidating dogs; of spaniels; and ends with a dialogue carried on during a day's sport.

The author remarked that while in Great Britain and Ireland it was not common for the pointers to fetch dead or wounded game, in America or other wooded countries this was an indispensable qualification on account of the immense cover and brush.

Most of his shooting near New York was done on the Bushy Plains on Long Island. The best dog he ever saw formerly belonged to General Birche, who had given him to a guide on Long Island. When the author knew him, the dog was thin from constant hunting, and so little excited about it, that after he had pointed the game he would sit calmly down on his haunches and wait for the hunter to come up.

When the British were occupying New York during the Revolution, there were many races run on Hempstead Plains, or Ascot Heath, as they called it temporarily. In November, 1780, three days of racing are advertised in *Rivington's Gazette*. On the first day was a Gentlemen's Purse of £65, and a purse for ponies of £15. On the second day was a Ladies' Subscription of £50, and one to be run for by women. On the last day was a Country Subscription Purse of £50.

Even more noteworthy than these details is the notice:

"Gentlemen fond of fox hunting will meet at Loosely's Kings Head Tavern at daybreak during the races."

After the Revolution, when Washington returned to Mount Vernon, his kennel, which had been badly broken up during the war, was reëstablished by a present of some stag hounds from Lafayette. These were very large and required liberal use of the whip thong, though Custis, the general's adopted son, remembered riding astride the largest, which was called Vulcan.

Between 1783 and 1785, Custis wrote, there were often three hunts a week in season. Breakfast was served by candlelight, Washington's regularly consisting of corn cake and milk, and by sunrise the hunters were in the saddle.

Billy Lee, the huntsman, rode Chinkling and, crouching almost flat on the horse's back, would rush through brakes or tangled woods at reckless speed. Washington usually rode Blueskin, and kept up with the hounds, generally being in at the death.

There were also paths cut in various directions through the woods for less expert riders and ladies.

The foxes then were grey, all except one famous black fox, which, after being chased seven or eight times unsuccessfully, was let alone. But Custis thought that the red fox might have made its way from Maryland across the Chesapeake in the cold winter of 1779-1780.

Washington's last hunt with hounds was in 1785, when he gave away his dogs. Later he built a park for deer, but did not hunt them.

One of the most startling advertisements of the period after the Revolution is a notice in the *City Gazette-Daily Advertiser*, of Charleston, South Carolina, October 13, 1795. This runs:

Notice

The Anniversary of the *Golf Club* will be held on Saturday next at the Club-House, on Harleston's Green where the members are requested to attend at one o'clock.

William Mulligan, Secretary.

October 13.

This was repeated the next Saturday with a change to "will be held this day."

J. B. Latrobe in 1796 found a billiard table in use in Virginia. Francis Baily, the astronomer, wrote that there were a dozen in Norfolk at that date.

Baily wrote that the Chesapeake was frequented in the shooting season by parties after canvasback ducks. He saw partridges shot in Washington City. In a bear hunt in Ohio they found the tree in which the bear was hibernating and cut it down to get him. In New Orleans, Sunday afternoon was given over to amusements. Billiards was common there. Gentlemen of the city often played in the orchestra of the theatre.

In 1793 was published Patrick Campbell's *Travels in the Interior Inhabited Parts of North America*. He had formerly been a head gamekeeper in Scotland and was particularly struck by the method used in America of calling the moose during the mating season. His account of this stratagem, which is probably the first to go into details, runs in part:

"The sportsman . . . . is provided with a slip of birch bark about a span broad, which he rolls up in the form of a funnel; and when the proper time of night comes, putting the small end of it to his mouth, he blows through it, and gives the call peculiar to this animal; if the moose is within hearing, he answers the call, and comes rushing through the wood with such rapidity and noise that he is heard at a considerable distance, all the young saplings, branches, or bushes giving way to his great strength in his career."

Campbell also related how a sportsman after caribou, carried a branch in front of him and advanced so stealthily that he was not noticed. If he either killed or missed entirely the caribou were not disturbed, but if he only wounded one and it whistled, all would take alarm and not be seen again that day.

There is little doubt that both the calling of moose as described by Campbell and the stalking of caribou were copied from Indian methods. The Indians were great imitators of the calls of different animals and birds, and exhibited the utmost skill in their stealthy approach upon game or their enemies.

Campbell describes how the bee hunter would locate a bee tree by burning beeswax on a stone to attract the bees, and putting honey surrounded by vermilion on another stone. When the bees sipped the honey and started for their tree, he would take the direction with his compass, and note the time it took the ones marked by the vermilion to return, which would give him an idea of the distance of the tree.

In the racing field, about 1790, the descendants of Medley were most successful. Belair was beaten only once, and that time by Gimcrack, also a son of Medley. Calypso, a sister of Belair, won thirteen out of fourteen races about 1795.

In 1796 new lines of blood came into prominence. Virago, daughter of The Sharks, won ten races. Leviathan, by Flag of Truce, was victorious in sixteen races in Virginia and Maryland between 1798 and 1800.

Horsemen were beginning to place great confidence in blood, and the performances of the various breeds were carefully watched, though the breeding and records were not as yet religiously registered or preserved in any stud book or archives.

THE EARLY NINETEENTH CENTURY

IN 1804 Alexander Wilson, later the author of the *American Ornithology*, made a hike with two companions from Philadelphia to Niagara. He kept a diary on the way, and in 1809 and 1810 wrote a poetic description of the trip, entitled *The Foresters*, for *The Port Folio*, a magazine. The poem is much truer to life than most poetry of that day, and in places is of high merit.

Several engravings which illustrate the poem touch upon hunting. One of these, entitled Hunters on the Susquehanna, depicts the party coming across a huge rattlesnake. The account of the incident in the poem runs as follows:

> There glistening lay, extended o'er the path,
> With steadfast piercing eyes, and gathering wrath,
> A large grim rattlesnake, of monstrous size,
> Three times three feet his length enormous lies;
> His pointed scales in regular rows engraved;
> His yellow sides with wreathes of dusky waved;
> Fixed to the spot, with staring eyes, we stood:
> He, slowly moving, sought the adjoining wood;
> Conscious of deadly power, he seemed to say,
> "Pass on; in peace let each pursue his way."
>
> But when th' uplifted musquet met his view,
> Sudden in sounding coils his form he threw.

[49]

Fierce from his center rose his flatten'd head,
With quivering tongue and eyes of fiery red,
And jaws extended vast, where threatening lay
The fangs of death in horrible array;
While poised above, invisible to view,
His whizzing tail in swift vibration flew.

The hunters took aim to shoot the reptile, but, rather quixotically, decided not to do so, on the ground that the rattlesnake had warned them before he struck.

Later in the journey, the landlord of the Shades of Death regaled them with many tales

Of panthers trapt — of wounded bears enraged;
The wolves and wildcats he had oft engaged;
The noble bucks his rifle had brought down —
How living rattlesnakes he had brought to town.
His dog's exploits — the glory of his kind,
Nero gashed by bears, and lame, and almost blind.

Notable among the stories told by the landlord was how one of his neighbors was startled by finding that he had not only caught a panther in his trap but that two others were waiting by it. Afraid to hazard a shot, he hurried home and loading another gun gave it to his wife who went back with him. When he raised his gun to shoot he was so nervous that he was afraid he would miss, but his wife bade him to rest the gun on her shoulder. This he did and killed the two free panthers with two shots. Curiously enough, the engraver in representing this adventure made the panthers look like jaguars.

But the day of the hunter and trapper was waning, as Wilson put it:

Here nature bounteous to excess has been,
Yet loitering hunters scarce a living glean.

The trapper's return, 1810

A hunter and his wife, 1812

[51]

At one trapper's hut where they slept, the owner came in from an absence of several days with spoil which Wilson describes as follows:

> Just as the dame her glowing hearth had cleared,
> The ragged owner of the hut appear'd,
> Laden with skins, his traps around him slung,
> Two dead raccoons across his shoulder hung,
> Muskrats and 'possums in his hands he bore,
> A large brown otter trail'd along the floor.

Yet it might have paid him better to have stayed at home, if he could have shot or trapped the wolves that had killed his calves while he was away. Altogether the backwoods were getting too settled for hunting but were still too wild for farming.

From 1808 until the year of his death in 1813, Wilson was engrossed in his *American Ornithology*, for which he travelled through the eastern states and south as far as New Orleans in gathering data and taking subscriptions.

There are many fine drawings from life in the volumes, but no pictures of hunting. There are, however, several remarks on the hunting of various game birds that should not be overlooked.

Wilson said that the great place for hunting the pinnated grouse was on the Bushy Plains of Long Island. This bird was popularly known as the heath hen, and was so designated in a New York law providing for a closed season in Suffolk and Queens Counties between April 1st and October 5th. The Chairman of the Assembly, who was no sportsman, read the title "For the preservation of the heathen," — and apparently thought it was to stop indiscriminate shooting of the Indians.

In the pairing season, which began in March, the tooting of the males could be heard for three miles. The males assembled by themselves, tooting, strutting, fighting, and if hunters could find the meeting place, they would build houses of boughs and wait for the males at daybreak. A pair sold in the New York market at from $3.75 to $5.00.

[53]

The ruffed grouse was called a partridge in the eastern states and a pheasant in Pennsylvania. A good dog would find it in the woods, where it would spring when the hunter was within a few yards and go whirring through the bushes and branches. Sometimes a number would be found upon a tree, and frequently several could be shot one after another, especially if the ones on the lower limbs were shot first, before the rest took flight. A pair sold in the Philadelphia market at about a dollar.

The quail, or bobwhite, in places also called the partridge, was frequently caught in cone-shaped traps, to the number of ten or fifteen at a time. In severe winters when caught this way they were sometimes bought by sportsmen who kept them over the winter and turned them loose in the spring.

Wilson corroborated the accounts of the passenger pigeon. He witnessed one flight that extended a mile in width and kept up for more than four hours.

A pigeon breeding place in a beechnut forest, near Shelbyville, Kentucky, extended about forty miles north and south and was several miles broad. There was a constant roar like thunder from millions of wings. As high as a hundred nests were in a tree, one squab to a nest. The hunters there sought particularly the squabs which grew almost as large as the old birds and were very fat and tender. Such a breeding place was very destructive to the forest, and sometimes killed thousands of acres of trees in a season.

Rail appeared in great numbers among the reeds of the Delaware, in August, and disappeared so suddenly at the end of the season that some people thought they lay buried in the mud over the winter. But Wilson demonstrated that in spite of their seemingly clumsy flight, they migrated, probably along the coast.

They were hunted in a light bateau, with a stout boatman to push it with a pole from twelve to fifteen feet long. The pole was made thicker at the lower end in order to prevent it from sinking into the mud. The shooting was done at high tide, which lessened the cover for the birds.

Shooting wolves, 1813

Bear hunting, 1813

[55]

The rails usually sprung singly, and made a short, slow flight during which they were easy to shoot. A hunter might get ten or twelve dozen in a tide.

Negroes on the James River sometimes hunted the rail with a fire which so dumbfounded the sora, as the rail was called there, that they could be knocked down with a paddle. This was much the same method used, according to the Reverend Andrew Burnaby, by the Indians in 1760.

The Canada goose was hunted by means of tamed Canada geese which honked as the wild ones flew over and drew them close enough to be shot by the hunters concealed nearby. They weighed from ten to twelve pounds and were sold in Philadelphia for from seventy-five cents to a dollar.

A farmer by the name of Platt on Long Island had a tamed goose which rose and joined a flock one fall, and with her family dropped down from a flock the next spring, and never afterwards made any effort to leave.

Canvasback ducks, which arrived on the Chesapeake and adjacent rivers about the middle of October, were decoyed by a dog playing along the shore. As put by Wilson: "The dog, if properly trained, plays backwards and forwards along the margin of the water, and the ducks observing his manœuvres, enticed perhaps by curiosity, gradually approach the shore, until they are sometimes within twenty or thirty yards of the spot where the hunter lies concealed, and from which he rakes them first in the water and then as they rise. This method is called tolling them in."

Mallard ducks were hunted with the aid of wooden decoys fastened at the length of a pole from a skiff which was covered with sedge or grasses. In the winter a hunter sometimes painted his canoe white and crept up toward the ducks unobserved amid the ice.

Sports in the cities are suggested by a detail in a view of Yale showing two students kicking a football in 1806, a broadside or handbill of a cock-fight in 1807, and an advertisement in the *Post* of a rowing race in 1811.

Rowing came into public prominence at that date (1811). First there was a race between a boat owned by the proprietors of the *Mercantile Advertiser* and built by John Baptist and one owned by Mr. Snyder, built by John Chambers. This was soon followed by a much-heralded rowing race between the Knickerbocker of New York and the Invincible of Long Island. The course, from Harsimus, N. J. to the flagstaff at the Battery, on that day was rough. The race was won by the Knickerbocker, which proved the better sea boat. This craft was thereupon deposited in Scudder's Museum as a model; it was later purchased by Barnum and burned in the fire that destroyed his Museum.

In 1819 *Foreign Field Sports*, illustrated by Atkinson, Clark, Manskirch, and others, was published in London. Among the many lithographs which are dated 1813 were several interesting ones on American subjects.

The frontispiece illustrated the adventure of a boy with wolves. When coming through the woods, bringing home some meat, he discovered that he was being trailed by a pack. He dropped one piece of meat after another to detain them, but finally had to flee for a deserted cabin. He managed to get upon the rafters as the wolves rushed through the doorway, and then succeeded in letting down the door and shutting them in. Breaking through the thatch, early in the morning, he saw a man going to work and sent for his father to bring his rifle and plenty of ammunition. This was done, and they killed all nine of the wolves from the roof.

The following customs were illustrated in lithographs that are spirited in action and evidently attempt to be true to the life:

Elk, according to the description, were either run down in the deep snow by hunters and dogs, or driven into a lake where they were met by hunters in canoes. Bears were frequently hunted by a dozen or twenty settlers in a posse, and after being brought to bay by the dogs, were killed by fusees or even by lances. On the shores of North America it was customary for navigators to put to shore and shoot deer on the fertile cliffs or slopes. On Lake Ontario, a fire was built on the prow of the boat, and the fish speared as they were attracted to the light.

Elk hunting, 1813

Woodcock shooting, 1830

[59]

In the decade before the War of 1812, racing was in full sway in New York, Pennsylvania, Maryland, Virginia, and the Carolinas.

In 1802 Expectation, by Bedford, won the sweepstakes at Richmond, running two miles in 3:47, and was thereupon sold by Colonel Tayloe for $4,000 to Colonel Alston, who renamed him Gallatin, and took him to South Carolina, where he was the head of the turf for several years.

As a whole, during this decade the blood of Diomed was in the ascendancy, his descendants, Peace Maker, Top Gallant, Florizel, Sir Archy, and Duroc being the most consistent winners. Peace Maker's time of two miles in 3:40 made in 1803, remained the record until 1829.

The get of Gabriel, particularly Post Boy and Oscar were also highly successful, both defeating First Consul which had won twenty-one races in New York, Pennsylvania and Maryland, and had challenged any horse in America.

In 1812 Pacolet, by Citizen, after winning at Richmond, was sold to General Andrew Jackson for $3,000.

In the racing states, racing was encouraged because it bettered the breed of horses, and horses were raised because they might win fame and money on the tracks. At the regular meetings purses were offered, but there were many special matches between horses that had or were beginning to have a reputation. Private betting was common at the established races, and inevitable at the special matches. The southern sportsman always took great pride in his favorite horse, and the proceeds of many a bale of cotton changed hands on the results of the races. Racing in the South offered excitement for the leisure class, and, as usual, some of them became deeply engrossed in it. In the North, racing supplied an outside interest for wealthy business men, but gradually developed more professional but not more rabid followers than in the South.

FIELD SPORTS

1820–1830

AN American bear hunt is pictured in an engraving in the *Sporting Magazine* for 1820. The American bear, it was explained, when closely pursued by dogs took to the water, where his physique enabled him to fight standing upright, and gave him a tremendous advantage over the dogs, which had to fight swimming. And woe to the dog which got within reach of his paws, which he handled with the skill of a boxer and the deadliness of a battle ax. But the hunters, aware of this, rushed to the aid of the dogs and dispatched him as soon as possible with a rifle shot.

The second of the American sportsman's handbooks was the *American Shooter's Manual*, stated to be by a gentleman of Philadelphia, and published there in 1827. This was in part a compilation from British originals, from the *Sportsman's Companion* and from Wilson's *Ornithology*.

The book dealt with shooting on the wing, which was stated to have been only recently developed in America. It advised the learner to practice this against the rail, a slow-flying bird. It described hunting dogs, and especially pointers and setters and their breaking, mostly after British methods. A moot point here was whether the dogs should be taught to bring in the game when shot, as usually done in America. Game birds were taken up separately, — the partridge, ruffed grouse, grouse, woodcock, snipe, rail, ducks, and turkey, the natural history being in part taken from Wilson's *Ornithology*. Of the engravings, the one on rail shooting was the most American.

A strictly native custom of attracting or "toleing" ducks was recorded much as described by Wilson, a hunter hiding behind a blind and keeping a dog retrieving chips along the shore. When the ducks out in the lake caught sight of the dog's efforts, they would become excited with curiosity and swim near to see what was going on.

Turkey gobblers were attracted by imitating the calls of their mates, and were usually shot with a rifle. This method of calling no doubt went back to Indian strategy.

The flintlock was going out and percussion caps coming in. The merits of the double barrel for fowling pieces were becoming recognized, though the gun was as yet in the hands of very few.

In the *American Turf Register*, which was founded in August, 1829, as a development of the *American Farmer*, was a mass of data on horses and racing, and various notes on miscellaneous sports. The first volume may be summarized to supply a cross section of American sport at that date:

New Associations to promote horse racing and breeding were the Hunting Park Association at Philadelphia to promote trotting, and the Mississippi Association. Memorials of well known sires, and racing calendars and results fulfilled the name of the magazine. On the Long Island course Bowery Boy defeated Stranger in 5:07 for two miles. The get of Eclipse won the two races they entered on the Union course, Long Island.

A new stop watch was announced. An amateur walked six miles in $58\frac{1}{2}$ minutes.

Fox chases were reported by the Baltimore Pack, the Terrett and Darne's hounds in Fairfax County, Virginia, and by the Ravensworth, Potomac, Annapolis, and Raleigh packs. Packs crossing each other kept on the trail of their own fox. There were several letters on the origin of the red fox.

Stags and deer were driven by dogs but shot by the hunters waiting at stands on the trails. A brush blind was also used to enable a hunter to approach within range of deer.

Tolling ducks was said to have started about 1800 from a hunter

Rail shooting on the Delaware, 1830

Rail, 1830

watching the effect of the antics of a red fox on the shore. A new flying kite was offered to attract flying geese or ducks.

The Schuylkill Fishing Company, which was founded in 1732, was soon to celebrate its centenary. Trout fishing in Vermont by two men produced 570 fish in nine hours.

Trolling for rock fish in the Susquehanna was thought to strike a different note. The "swivels and figures" had to be made by the blacksmith of the neighborhood. Ray or devil fish were caught near Beaufort, South Carolina, measuring eighteen feet across the back.

A great cock main was held at Harrisburg, February 11-12, 1830, for $1,000 and $100 for each fight. Spirited wolf hunting with dogs and guns was reported from Fort Dearborn.

So much for a glimpse of a year's sport.

The description of the wolf hunt near Fort Dearborn in December, 1829, is interesting not only as an early account of such a chase, but because it took place within the present limits of Chicago and perhaps within the present "Loop."

"We principally hunt in this section the prairie wolf," wrote the author of the article in the *American Turf Register*. The party set forth with four couples of dogs and a leash of greyhounds. At the little woods on the east side of the Chicago River they started a wolf which was seen and chased by the hounds. The wolf kept ahead for a time and then when becoming pressed attempted to cross the frozen stream. But while still on the ice, he was nabbed by old Nero, the black greyhound, who held him until the other dogs came up and helped in the kill.

They hung the head of the miscreant on a tree as a warning to his pack, and set forth to rout out another. A second wolf was seen at a distance and the dogs took after him at full speed. After a chase of about a mile, old Nero caught up with the wolf, and, running into him full speed, knocked him over and seized him by the throat before he could scramble to his feet. As usual old Nero did the lion's share of the fighting, but the other dogs came up in time for the kill.

[67]

Still another wolf was tracked by scent, followed for some distance, and then seen and chased by sight. The author of the article, J. G. F., and another of the party were thrown from their horses into the snow, as the horses broke through the icy crust and stumbled, but the dogs caught the wolf and after a big fight, in which they were pretty well marked up, killed it.

The Cabinet of Natural History and American Rural Sports, which was published in Philadelphia in 1830-1832, contains many lithographs of birds and beasts, a few of which represent hunting.

Woodcock shooting was done with the aid of a dog on moist and usually woody grounds. The bird rose so sluggishly it was easy to shoot in a clearing, but thickets, where it was commonly found, made it difficult. Since the woodcock fed at twilight, this was thought to be the most productive period in which to hunt it. It was already becoming scarce in New Jersey and was protected there between July 1st and January 31st.

There is an interesting lithograph of rail shooting but the account of it is taken largely from Wilson's *Ornithology*.

Foxhunting was described as particularly a southern sport:

"From Maryland south this (foxhunting) has always been the favorite amusement of the sportsmen, by whom it is followed with a keenness and perseverance, which show at once its fascinating tendency. There are, however, Foxhunters in almost every state, but their number is so small, and excursions comparatively so few that it may properly be called a *Southern Sport*."

It is stated that the United Bowmen of Philadelphia was founded as an association in the fall of 1828, and that at that time the art was so far forgotten that the company had to copy its equipment from bows and arrows in the museums. Later, equipment was ordered from London and received in March, 1829. The initiation was $5.00 and the dues fifty cents a month.

A good conception of angling a century ago is given in the appendix to Jerome Van Crowninshield Smith's *Fishes of Massachusetts*, 1833.

Killing two deer with a bird gun, 1833

The United Bowmen of Philadelphia, 1838

He made the classification, for angling purposes, of pond trout, brook trout, and sea trout. His general principle as to bait was that it should be, or imitate, the food of the fish at that time and place. In angling for trout in the Sebago Pond, near Portland, Maine, he used a long, stout salmon rod, with rings to guide from 80 to 100 yards of silk and hair line. He had a single, not a multiple, brass reel attached to the short, stout butt; mackeral hooks attached to gut, and a musket ball to give weight.

He trolled for the fish, using as bait a shiner or smelt, which was the food of the fish. Artificial flies had seldom or never been tried there.

As a matter of fact, artificial flies, as it is easy to see from his account, were just beginning to come in, and to be introduced chiefly by anglers who had become accustomed to them in England. In Great Britain they had flies for every month in the year, but in America only a few standard varieties were purchasable. Smith's remarks on the use of artificial flies in angling for brook trout run as follows:

"There is scarcely a brook or river but there is sure to be located at a convenient distance from it, some veteran angler from the *old country*, who enjoys the undisturbed monopoly of its finny treasures. He scorns the vulgar bait. He enjoys the sport and exults in its success, according as it requires an exertion of his skill. . . .

"There are not only individuals of whom we speak, but others who availing themselves of all the information to be acquired from books and experience, are fully aware that fly-fishing is the perfection of angling."

Smith's description of the rod employed for brook trout is particularly interesting if contrasted mentally with that in use to-day:

"The wood is of hickory; it is twelve and a half feet long; it has but three joints, which are ferruled only on one end for the sake of lightness; the butt is solid, very large in the hand, and tapers very suddenly; into the end of it a spike of five inches in length, thin like a knife, is made to screw, for the purpose of supporting the rod upright in the ground, as this is a position in which it is least exposed to danger . . . . finally, when put together it weighs but thirteen or fourteen ounces without the spike.

[71]

"A reel or winch is indispensable; it should be such as is called *multiplying*, with which advantage is taken in exhausting the fish, by winding up the line with greater rapidity, whenever it becomes relaxed. The line should be about thirty yards long, and made of patent silk and hair, either of a green or gray color; smaller lines, made of that indispensable material *gut* are also necessary; these are called '*casting* lines' and sometimes '*foot lengths*', and are attached, as occasion may require, to the principal line, for the purpose of falling with less violence on the water."

Sea trout were fished for at the mouths of streams where the water was brackish. The bait used was the shrimp in spring and the minnow in summer, which, in fact, were the common food of the fish at such seasons.

The Spirit of the Times, 1832

SPORTING LITERATURE

1830-1860

THIS era was remarkable for the founding of the first sporting periodicals in the United States and for the development of the first sporting writers.

The founder of the *American Turf Register* was John Stuart Skinner, whose life had many notable incidents. Born in Maryland on Washington's birthday, 1788, he fitted himself for the law and began practice at twenty-one. Only three years afterwards he was made government agent to receive and forward the ocean mails, to furnish vessels with supplies and see that nothing occurred harmful to the Republic or to enemy ships admitted under a flag of truce. A little later he was made the agent for prisoners of war, and in 1813 was transferred from Annapolis to Baltimore. He learned of the approach of the enemy's ships of war and rode ninety miles in a night to warn the forts, the British in retaliation burning his estate. He was with Francis Scott Key on his mission to the British warship when Key wrote the Star Spangled Banner. From 1816 to 1840 he was postmaster at Baltimore.

In 1819 he established the *American Farmer*. Five years later he entertained Lafayette while in Baltimore on his second visit to this country, and was made the agent to handle the estate of 24,000 acres presented to Lafayette by Congress.

In August, 1829, Skinner published in Baltimore the first number of the *American Turf Register*, the first sporting magazine in the country. It was concerned principally with horse racing and especially with running races, but contained various articles and notes on other sports.

[75]

Ten years later he sold the *American Turf Register* to William Trotter Porter, and soon turned his attention chiefly to farm papers.

The new owner of the *American Turf Register* had been interested in sporting periodicals for several years. He was born at Newbury, Vermont, in 1807, and was educated at Dartmouth College, though he was not graduated. He was on the *Farmer's Herald* at St. Johnsbury, Vermont, became an associate editor at Norwich, and then moved to New York and became superintendent of a printing plant, where he engaged Horace Greeley as a compositor.

On December 10th, 1831, he issued in New York the first number of the *Spirit of the Times*, a weekly racing paper, with notices on other sports. It was not financially successful and in a few months was merged with the *Traveller*, Porter being in charge of the sporting department. From 1832 to 1834 he was on other papers, then in 1835 he purchased the *Traveller* and *Spirit of the Times* from C. J. B. Fisher, and on January 3rd, 1835, began to issue it again as the *Spirit of the Times*, making the numbering continuous from 1831, which is the secret of the so-called lost volumes of the *Spirit of the Times*. His aim was to raise the standing of racing and to a lesser extent of other sport, and his weekly contained articles by such noteworthy contributors as Thomas B. Thorpe, and "Frank Forester." He was well known to the sporting public, and his tall figure, six feet four in height, was prominent at all important events.

In 1839 he purchased the *American Turf Register* from John Stuart Skinner and moved it to New York, but it was eventually found that there was not sufficient demand for both a weekly and a monthly, and in 1845 the *Turf Register* was reduced to a mere summary of racing events, or racing calendar.

Probably the most influential contributor on field sports to these sporting magazines was Henry William Herbert, who wrote under the name of Frank Forester. His father was a son of the Earl of Carnavon, and Henry William was graduated from Cambridge in 1830 with honors. On the loss of his property the next year through a dishonest trustee, he came to America and began to teach the classics in New York in an institute making a specialty of these subjects.

He wrote various essays for the budding American magazines but could get no pay for them. In 1834 he wrote a novel, *The Brothers*, but did not receive any important financial return from it, and his historical work, *Cromwell*, published in 1837, paid no better.

In 1839, however, he wrote for the *Turf Register* a series, *A Week in the Warwick Woodlands*, which attracted immediate attention. From that time on he contributed sporting articles to the *Spirit of the Times*, the *American Turf Register*, *Graham's Magazine*, and occasionally to other periodicals.

Sports in America had been highly utilitarian, or looked askance at, and not considered worthy of the attention of a serious-minded citizen; Herbert introduced something of the English point of view of sport for sport's sake with a chance given the game.

Herbert's end was dramatic. In 1858 he married again, but his wife left his New Jersey home when she learned of his previous dissipations. Soon afterward he had a grand dinner prepared in New York City, invited his old friends, only one of whom came, and shot himself before the mirror.

Another of the sporting writers was William P. Hawes, who wrote under the name of J. Cypress, Jr. Born in New York City in 1803, he was graduated at Columbia, studied law, and practiced with John Anthon. He wrote essays and political articles, but more successfully sketches for the new sporting magazines. After his early death in 1842, these were collected in a volume edited by Herbert.

The great West and the Indians were beginning in the thirties to excite an interest more scientific than that of the fur traders.

In 1832-1834 Prince Maximilian of Wied, a German naturalist who had already made a journey into Brazil, headed a large expedition to the Upper Missouri, and later published an account of it, including some splendid views he had painted by Mr. Bodmer, the artist.

The prince wrote of their first kill of a grizzly bear as follows:
"The sight of this first bear chase was interesting and we that remained as spectators on deck awaited the result with impatience. Dechamp, a bold and experienced hunter and excellent marksman, was put on shore and crept unperceived along the strand, till he got to a branch of a tree about eighty paces from the bear, in order, in case of need, to intercept his retreat to the thickets. The ravenous bear sometimes raised his colossal head, looked around him, and then greedily returned to his repast; doubtless because the wind was in our favor, and these animals are not remarkably quick sighted. The boat had got to within fifty paces when the pieces were leveled. Mr. Mitchell fired the first mortal shot, behind the shoulder blade. The other shots followed in quick succession, on which the bear rolled over, uttered fearful cries, tumbled about ten steps forwards, scratched the wounded places furiously with his paws, and turned several times completely over."

In taking part in a buffalo hunt near Fort McKenzie, the Prince rode twenty miles until the party reached an eminence whence they could examine the prairie with a telescope. Several small groups of buffaloes were sighted, and the hunters rode for the largest group. When they approached near enough, they made a regular cavalry charge, but the bulls galloped off at a great rate. The buffaloes separated and the riders divided to follow them. Wied followed one bull into a small ravine, where with two other horsemen he shot him. The bull threatened to charge and did advance several times, nor did he fall until he received perhaps twenty bullets. Wied wrote that the prairie hunters were much more skillful, because they knew just where to shoot. They were also very quick at reloading, because they dropped the moistened ball directly on the powder with no wadding between.

The greatest portrayer of the West was George Catlin. His mother, when a girl eight years of age, had been captured by the Indians in the fall of Forty Fort. Catlin practiced law but became more noted as a portrait painter. Then in 1829 he went among the Indians and made portraits

Shooting a grizzly bear on the Upper Missouri, 1832

Killing a deer, 1833

[79]

and pictures of them during part of each year for the next ten years. His drawings included about six hundred items, and his paintings, which he exhibited in a collection, were as many. Having lost in a speculation, Catlin hypothecated his paintings, which were later presented by Mrs. Joseph Harrison to the United States National Museum.

Catlin took part in an exciting buffalo hunt near the mouth of the Yellowstone River, which he described in part as follows:

"The horses — when 'approaching,' — which is, all of us abreast, upon a slow walk, and in a straight line toward the herd, until they discover us and run, — all seem to have caught entirely the spirit of the chase, for the laziest nag amongst them prances with an elasticity in his step — champing his bit, his ears erect, his eyes strained out of his head, and fixed upon the game before him, whilst he trembles under the saddle of his rider. In this way we carefully and silently marched, until within some forty or fifty rods; when the herd, discovering us, wheeled and laid out their course in a mass. At this instant we started! and all must start for no one could check the fury of those steeds at that moment of excitement. I had discovered a huge bull whose shoulders towered above the whole band, and I picked my way through the crowd to get along-side of him. I went not for meat but for a *trophy*: I wanted the head and horns. I dashed along through the thundering mass, as they swept away over the plain, scarcely able to tell whether I was on a buffalo's back or my horse — hit and hooked and jostled about until at length I found myself along-side of my game, when I gave him a shot as I passed him. I saw guns flash in several directions about me, but I heard them not. Mons. Chardon had wounded a stately bull — when the bull instantly turned and receiving the horse upon his horns, the ground received poor Chardon, who made a frog's leap of some twenty feet or more over the bull's back."

Luckily neither horse nor rider was killed, and Catlin got a chance to sketch his buffalo.

He tells also of a method of flagging or decoying antelopes, which he witnessed on the upper Missouri. The hunter got as near to the antelopes as possible without being seen, and then used the following ruse:

"When he (the hunter) has been discovered, he has only to elevate, above the tops of the grass, his red or yellow handkerchief on the end of his gun-rod, which he sticks in the ground, and to which they are sure to advance, though with great coyness and caution."

Notable among the writers on sport in the years before the Civil War was Thomas Bangs Thorpe. He was born in Westfield, Massachusetts, in 1815 and attended Wesleyan University, where he became known for his painting and writing. Soon afterward, in 1836, he went to Louisiana, from where about 1841 he began to send humorous and local-color sporting descriptions to the *American Turf Register*. His Big Bear of Arkansas attracted wide attention, and his description of wildcat hunting was of vivid interest.

He served as a colonel in the Mexican War, and then became an editor on first one and then another New Orleans paper. In 1854 he published *Tom Owen the Bee Hunter*, which contains a number of his sketches. One of these on wild turkey hunting is probably the best description of calling the gobbler to his doom. It dramatizes the hour-long struggle between the sex-call and caution, and helps us to appreciate the artistry and infinite patience of the hunter. From Thorpe's description, the turkey caller earned his shot. Other sketches are on shooting fish with an arrow, alligator killing, buffalo chasing, opossum hunting, and the influences of fire in stupefying woodcocks at night.

In 1859 Thorpe became publisher and editor of the *Spirit of the Times*, but he continued to contribute now and then to magazines such as *Blackwood's*, the *Knickerbocker*, and *Harpers*.

Another writer on sports in the fifties was Charles Wilkins Webber, who had a short but adventurous life. He was born in Russelville, Kentucky, in 1819, and at the age of nineteen went to Texas where he served as a ranger.

He returned to Kentucky to study medicine and then attended Princeton Theological Seminary but was not graduated. After being on

Flagging antelopes. Catlin, 1841

A buffalo hunt. Catlin, 1841

[83]

a paper in New York, he led an expedition in 1849 to Colorado, in which their horses were stolen by the Comanche Indians. He helped to form a company to introduce camels into the southwest, but the plan was never developed. In the winter of 1855-56 he joined William Walker in his filibustering expedition into Central America, and took part in the Battle of Rivas, but was killed not long afterward.

Webber's most important work on sport was *The Hunter-Naturalist*, published in 1851. An interesting chapter in this is on hunting the grey fox in the South, in which he distinguishes between the rough and ready methods there, and the punctiliousness of an English hunt. The start of the hunt was described by Webber as follows:

"In the older southern states the modes of hunting the Grey Fox are pretty much alike. To the sound of winding horns the neighboring gentry collect at an appointed place, each accompanied by his favorite dogs, and usually a negro driver to manage them and keep them from starting a deer. Mounted on fine horses, accustomed to the sport, they send in the hounds and await the start, chatting in a group, collected in some by-road, or some high spot of open ground from which they can hear every sound borne upon the breeze.

"The trail he has left during his nocturnal rambles being struck, the hounds are encouraged by the voices of their drivers to as great speed as the devious course it leads them will permit."

The trail of the fox was followed at headlong speed, and after an hour or two he was probably driven to a hole in which he might be left, or to a tree whence he was probably dislodged and given another chance.

Webber wrote that they lost one fox at a fence corner so often that even the hounds, when they picked up his scent, became discouraged and listless, as if they knew it was hopeless to chase him. Webber finally hid near the place, and saw the fox leisurely mount the rail fence, run along it for a way and then make a long leap to a tree, which had a hole near the top of the trunk. Webber let him get away with the trick, but later another foxhunter discovered it, and had the tree chopped down.

Among sources giving a conception of the history of early American sport the lithographs of Nathaniel Currier must not be overlooked. Lithography had been experimented with by Bass Otis in Boston about 1820 and by William S. and John Pendleton in Boston in 1824.

The latter firm took Nathaniel Currier in as an apprentice in 1828. Five years later Currier was working in Philadelphia, but in 1834 moved to New York, and with Stodart bought out Pendleton. Currier dated his business from that year, 1834, when it was located at 137 Broadway, though he bought out Stodart the next year and moved to 1 Wall Street. In 1836-37 he was at 148 Nassau, and from 1838 to 1856 was at 152 Nassau and 2 Spruce Street. Ives did not become a member of the firm until 1857.

In spite of the fact that Currier was in business in 1834, his sporting prints scarcely began to appear for about ten years. His early racing lithographs that have come to light are those representing The Dutchman, 1839; Peytona defeating Fashion, 1845; Trustee trotting twenty miles in an hour, 1848; Daniel D. Tompkins versus Blanc Negre, 1849; and the Star of the Road, 1849.

Historically his most important racing subjects of the early fifties were Lady Suffolk, 1850; Grey Eagle, 1850; Ripton and Confidence, 1850; Centerville and Black Douglas, 1853; A Brush on the Road, 1853; Flora Temple and Highland Maid, 1853; Lexington, 1855; and several others of Flora Temple versus other competitors.

Of hunting pictures, only a few on foxhunting, dated 1846, and one on rabbit hunting dated 1849, are before 1850. Lithographs of 1852 depict partridge, quail, rail, wild duck, and woodcock shooting. These subjects are repeated in 1855, and to this date belongs his lithograph on deer shooting at Shattagee.

The Trout Stream is dated 1852, and Catching Trout, 1854.

There are several lithographs of the yacht America, 1851; one of the Maria, 1852; and one of the New York Yacht Club Regatta, 1854.

Between 1855 and 1860 the lithographs are far more numerous.

A bear hunt, 1840

An American fox hunt, 1851

[87]

Buffalo hunting, 1840

An American hunter's camp, 1840

Among a dozen on racing, the most noteworthy historically are probably those of Ethan Allen and George M. Patchen, 1858; Flora Temple and Princess, 1859; Trotting Cracks on the Snow, 1858; Lady Woodruff on the Union Course, Long Island, 1857; Mac and Zachary Taylor, 1857; and Prince and Lantern, 1857.

A good shooting series dates from 1857, and includes On a Point, Flushed, A Chance for Both Barrels, and Retrieving. Camping Out belongs to 1856 and Life in the Country to 1859. Two lithographs of 1856 touch on trout fishing at Chateaugay Lake and bass fishing at McComb's Dam.

Currier's earliest known lithograph of a prize fight is of the Heenan-Sayers fight, 1860; and his first of baseball dates from 1862.

These lithographs on American subjects are important historically not only because they are original documents for the period, but because there are so few pictures available from that date. One may consider the drawing, in certain instances, none too good, and the colors usually garish, but they are vivid in action and essentially true to the life of their epoch, with a fidelity of which the artist himself was probably not fully aware.

FIELD SPORTS

1830-1860

AMONG sporting items of the thirties, we find an account of falconry carried on at Fairfax, Virginia, in 1830, by the Reverend Mr. Broders, who expatiated upon his hawks, Death and the Devil, in a technical jargon that was an unknown tongue to his visitors. He seemed to be an isolated anachronism brought down from the previous century.

The next year we get a description from Louisiana of shooting grassees which turn out to be the northern king bird fattened up on the abundant seeds of the South. From the upper Mississippi comes a narrative about a wolf chase on the ice. At Danville, Kentucky, deer were shot by still-hunting on foot. In a similar way Captain Mason and his party wrote in 1833 of "bouncing deer" in the American bottoms, by entering their haunts on horseback and shooting them as they bounded from their covers. At the same time appear notes of shooting fish and of hunting badgers in the West.

In Georgia bulls grew so wild that General C. R. Floyd speared one now and then, as they speared boars in Europe.

Near Cincinnati ducks were hunted by wading in the shoal ponds made in the woods of Ohio by the overflow of the rivers, and the hunters returned to the city on the canal boats. Turkeys were driven by a line of hunters, but, in the case narrated, the plan was not a success because the flintlocks got wet. The Cincinnati Independent Shooting Club, which was formed in 1832, for their contest throughout the season assigned a value to each sort of game as follows:

Deer	50	Swan	50
Bear	50	Goose	25
Grouse	25	Brant	25
Turkey	20	Canv. Bk	10
Pheasant	10	Redhd	8
Curleu	10	Blkhd	8
Woodck	5	Mallard	4
Plover	2	Wood dk	4
Snipe	2	Bunty	4
Rabbt	2	Teal	3
Quail	1	Rail	1

In the winter of 1835-1836, 157 wolves were chased down by hunters and dogs within the present limits of Chicago. In Arkansas the biggest game hunted were bears and panthers. Wisconsin was teeming with deer and wild fowl. Artificial fly fishing was becoming more common in the East.

In 1839 "Frank Forester" started his "Week in the Warwick Woodlands," and in 1840 "J. Cypress, Jr." began his "Week at Fire Islands, Long Island." An account of the use of a light in hunting deer was given by Audubon in 1841, while T. B. Thorpe wrote that woodcocks were so blinded by a light that they could be knocked down by a pole. An article from Louisiana described wild cat hunting as the most exciting sport.

In the last few volumes of the *American Turf Register*, we find several items on field sports that should not be passed by. In 1842 the Cincinnati Independent Shooting Club tried trap shooting of live pigeons; a traveller described how he was lost with his horse on the prairie and chased by wolves, and an account of salmon fishing came from Nova Scotia. In 1843 appear descriptions of wolf hunting on the ice of the upper Mississippi, and of hunting and deer stalking in Canada. From the last year in which the *Register* was a magazine, 1844, come accounts of deer hunting in Texas and of a walk amongst wild turkeys there.

Caribou showing fight, 1846

Moose hunting, 1859

[93]

A portage, 1858

A fight with wild cats, 1866

A hunter's adventure with two wildcats is illustrated in *Leslie's Weekly* in 1856. R. B. Simmons, who was out hunting about twenty miles from St. Louis with a couple of hounds and only a shotgun, heard a deep bay from the dogs and saw a big cat on a limb. He shot at it with birdshot and it fell from the limb. It was attacked by the dogs but soon drove them to seek protection with their master. In the meantime he had reloaded, and now fired again, killing the cat. He again reloaded and advanced to examine the wildcat, when he was shocked to see the mate about thirty feet away. He started to put on a percussion cap and the wildcat leaped fifteen feet toward him. The dogs, without more ado, fled. Remembering the tales he had heard of the power of the human eye over animals, he stared at the crouching wildcat, and grabbing hold of the dead one, slowly backed up, keeping his eyes on his foe. The wildcat followed him foot by foot as he retreated step by step, but did not go beyond the woods.

From *Leslie's* in 1858 comes a drawing of roping a grizzly bear in southern California. A number of cowboys with their horses and lariats surrounded him and one after another lassoed him, finally getting him so entangled in the rawhide ropes that he was helpless and could be killed with a knife.

A grizzly bear hunter there killed grizzlies with a rifle that was discharged with a pull on a piece of meat, as well as by his own handling. He had three hundred gallons of bear oil on hand, worth from eight to ten dollars a gallon.

In the East men were already beginning to seek recreation in the summer by going camping. In 1858 Agassiz, Emerson, and Lowell had a camp in the Adirondacks, where they chopped trees for exercise, fished for dinner, and talked for mutual enlightenment. They were visited by F. S. Stallkneck, the writer, and Charles E. Whitehead, the artist, who portrayed the camp and the portage nearby in an article in *Leslie's Weekly*. The portage was described as follows: "The second portage is reached about one o'clock. It is near two miles long, — a very bad soggy road, up and down rugged hills, fallen trees lying across the narrow footpath."

The canoe was carried by the guide and the visitors had enough to do to carry their own equipment.

Moose, according to an account in *Leslie's*, were hunted in Canada principally in March or September. In March they were chased when the snow had begun to melt in the daytime and freeze at night, which produced a crust through which the moose would break and thus be impeded. The men on snowshoes and the dogs could keep on top of the snow, and after a considerable run catch up with the game.

In the rutting season, which began in September, the bull moose was called by imitating the female. They were also stalked in autumn and winter, but not so easily, as their haunts were liable to be marshy in autumn and snow-covered in winter.

In 1860 the Prince of Wales visited Canada and the United States and among other diversions was taken out on the prairies to shoot prairie chickens, at a place chosen near Dwight, Illinois. The party rose at 5 a.m. and was driven in four carriages to a favorable spot. There, with the aid of a number of "small, lithe dogs," they divided into parties and proceeded to beat for game, each trying to bag the most chickens.

Luncheon was served under a tree near a cabin, and with a washbench for a table. The Prince's party killed sixty birds, but only half of them were prairie chickens, so they lost to Lord Hinchenbrook's party, which got thirty-five chickens.

The Prince of Wales and his companions shooting prairie chickens

The yacht America, 1851

The America winning the cup, 1851

[98]

ROWING AND YACHTING

1820-1860

IN the twenties rowing again excited great public interest, and important matches followed one another year after year.

The racing boats were known by name and in some cases became famous. We read of the New York defeating the American Star, and of the Whitehall beating the Richmond of Staten Island, for $1,000 and before 40,000 spectators; but the most celebrated of all these races was the international contest between the American Star and the champion gig of the British frigate, Hussar. Captain Harris of the Hussar, hearing of the prowess of the Whitehallers, challenged them to a race against his gig, Sudden Death, and was promptly taken up. The race was arranged to start from off Bedloe's Island, go up the Hudson to Hoboken, and return to the Battery flagstaff.

The Americans were represented by the American Star, built by John and William Chambers and rowed by Cornelius Cammeyer, Alfred Cammeyer, Richard Robbins, and Charles Beaty, with John Palmerton, coxswain. Their uniform consisted of a white guernsey, a blue handkerchief, and blue pants.

The American Star won handily before immense crowds of spectators that lined the Hudson and filled Battery Park. The next night the two crews appeared in racing costume on the stage of the old Park Theater, and were given a great ovation.

Later the American Star carried Lafayette from Whitehall to an entertainment at Colonel Hunt's in Jersey City. It was then presented to Lafayette and sent by him to Havre to improve French rowing.

[99]

The Castle Garden Boat Club Association was organized in 1834 and was a combination of several amateur rowing clubs. It held a regatta once a year for the next eight years, the course being around Bedloe's Island. There was also an Independent Boat Club Association in which the clubs were more loosely bound together.

Nor was rowing confined by any means to New York. At Philadelphia in 1835, the Sylph beat the Imp, traversing three and a half miles in ten minutes, fifteen seconds. At St. Mary's, Georgia, the Goddess of Liberty, thirty-two feet long with six oars, defeated the narrow Devil's Darning Needle, over a half-mile course in two minutes, twenty seconds.

There were regattas at Newburgh and Poughkeepsie in 1837. In New York in 1836 the celebrated six-oared Wave won the regatta around Bedloe's Island, about five and a half miles in thirty-one minutes.

Betting came in, and in 1838 the Disowned of the Independent Boat Club Association defeated the Washington of Poughkeepsie for $1,000; but soon afterward had the $1,000 taken away from it by the Spark of New York.

In 1838 George Steers, who afterward designed the America, built a four-oared racing boat with out-riggers. This was thirty feet long but weighed only one hundred and forty pounds, and with four oarsmen and a coxswain drew only four inches of water.

Rowing entered Harvard in 1843 when William Weeks of the Class of '44 purchased a four-oared boat and formed a crew for it. In 1845 members of the Class of '46 purchased the Star, an eight-oared racing boat, changing the name to Oneida, and manned it from the class.

The Yale, a racing boat of six oars, was bought by members of the Junior class in 1844. Boats from the two colleges met in the regatta at Lake Winnepesaukee in 1852, but though the crews and boats were from the colleges they did not officially represent them. In that race, for example, a crew and boat from the Class of 1853, Harvard, defeated three boats and crews from Yale. The Freshman class of the University of Pennsylvania formed a boat club in 1854, though the University had none.

In 1855 the Harvard boats Iris, eight-oared, and the Y. Y., four-oared, defeated both the Nereid and Nautilus, six-oared, from Yale. The Harvard boats were rowed without a coxswain, being guided by the bow oar.

At the first regatta of the College Union, held on Lake Quinsigamond, near Worcester, July 26, 1859, the Harvard and Avon, from Harvard, raced the Yale and the Atalanta from Brown, the Harvard winning with the Yale second.

The very next day, however, in the Citizens' Regatta at the same place, the Yale, rowing with a coxswain and near the shore, defeated the Harvard, which was rowed without a coxswain and farther out in the lake where it was rougher.

At about this time rowing clubs for comradeship and social purposes began to be organized in the waterfront cities. The Atalanta Boat Club of New York was founded in 1848, and the Union Boat Club of Boston in 1851. In 1858 the Schuylkill Navy was formed in Philadelphia by a combination of the Keystone, Excelsior, University, Bachelors, and other clubs.

In 1851 there was a much-talked-of sculling match for $500 between William Decker of the East River and James Lee of the North River, both "celebrated oarsmen." An "immense number of people" gathered at the Battery and large amounts of money were bet. The race was around Bedloe's Island, a distance of about five miles, and was won by Decker by perhaps three hundred yards.

Joshua Ward, who was born at Newburgh in 1838 and was one of four brothers, all noted oarsmen, won the championship belt at the Staten Island Regatta in 1859, rowing five miles in 35:10.

The pleasure yachts in the United States at the beginning of the nineteenth century were isolated personal hobbies, and there were no yacht clubs. Captain George Crowninshield of Salem, Massachusetts, who at the age of twenty was captain of a ship sailing to China and later became a ship designer and builder for his firm, in 1801 built a twenty-two-ton yacht, which in 1812 became a privateer in the war. At the end of the war, he constructed a pleasure schooner of almost two hundred tons which he named Cleopatra's Barge, after her historic craft. With this he sailed to the Mediterranean, but died soon after his return, and the schooner was sold for the coastwise trade.

Another New England yacht of that date was owned by Thomas Doubleday of Boston and sailed by him around Cape Cod Bay. In 1834 R. B. Forbes designed the Sylph for John P. Cushing of Boston. This was thought to be very fast but was challenged in 1835 by the Wave, owned by John C. Stevens of Hoboken, and defeated in a race off Boston.

In 1836, George Steers, then only seventeen years of age, built a seventeen-foot sailboat, the Martin Van Buren, and challenged the much-fancied Gladiator. The course was from the Battery to Fort Washington and return. The Gladiator was thought the fastest yacht on the Hudson and was sailed by William Bennett, but the Martin Van Buren, which Steers sailed himself, won handily. Steers became a naval architect and was closely associated with John C. Stevens.

John C. Stevens, son of the famous engineer and inventor, and himself an engineer of note, had experimented with boats from his boyhood. His miniature Dive and bothersome Trouble, and his catamaran, Double-Trouble, were largely experimental; his well-known Gimcrack was the first of the fin-keeled yachts.

It was on the Gimcrack, off the Battery, New York, that the New York Yacht Club was founded, July 29, 1844. At this organization meeting were present John C. Stevens of the Gimcrack, William Edgar of the Cygnet, John C. Jay of the La Coquilla, George L. Schuyler of the Dream, James C. Waterbury of the Minna, Louis A. Depau of the Mist, James Rogers of the Ida and George B. Rollins of the Petrol.

Mr. Stevens was chosen as commodore, and the newly organized club made a cruise to Newport. At the first regular election of officers, March 17, 1845, Mr. Stevens was elected commodore, an office which he continued to hold for more than a decade. Hamilton Wilkes was elected vice-commodore; George B. Rollins, corresponding secretary; John C. Jay, recording secretary; and William Edgar, treasurer. The first home of the club was a wooden structure in the Elysian Fields, Hoboken, near the commodore's residence. The club's first annual regatta was held in June, 1848.

In 1851 the schooner, America, was built for Commodore John C. Stevens by the now famous naval architect, George Steers, with the purpose of sending her to England to contest with the yachts there. She had a long, sharp bow, a width greatest a third of the way from the bow, and flat-trimmed sails.

She arrived at Cowes July, 1851, and offered to sail any yacht a race for from $1,000 to $50,000. This was accepted by Robert Stephenson, but before that race came off the America entered the regatta of the Royal Yacht Squadron for a cup valued at a hundred sovereigns. The interest in the foreign yacht and in the race was intense and widespread, and the Queen and Prince Albert came out to witness the event. *The Illustrated London News* described the start of the race as follows: "The start was effected splendidly, the yachts breaking away like a field of race horses; the only laggard was the America, which did not move for a second or so after the others. Steamboats, shore boats, and yachts of all sizes buzzed along on each side of the course, and spread away for miles over the rippling seas, — a sight such as the Adriatic never beheld in all the pride of Venice; such, beaten though we are, as no other country in the world could exhibit; while it is confessed that anything like it was never seen here."

At the end of the first quarter of an hour, three yachts were still ahead of the America, then she speedily advanced to the front. Off Sandown Bay she carried away her jib-boom, but while her competitors gained they did not approach her. Off Ventnor, the America was a mile ahead of the Aurora, her nearest rival. Rounding St. Catherine's Point in a moderate breeze even the Aurora dropped out of sight. At The Needles the America saluted the Victoria and Albert Royal Yacht, and at 6 p.m. the Aurora was from five to six miles astern. Thousands were still watching on the shore from West Cowes to past the Castle when at 8:37 the gun from the flagship announced the America's arrival. The Aurora came in twenty-one minutes later.

The America sailed from Cowes to Osborne to be inspected by the Queen and Prince Albert, who were shown about by Commodore Stevens and Colonel Hamilton.

The first race had been sailed against a squadron, but on August 28th, the America sailed a match race, forty miles out and return, against the Titania, a hundred-ton iron schooner owned by the famous engineer, Robert Stephenson, and thought to be the fastest of the British yachting fleet. The America won by a long distance. She was soon afterward bought by Lord de Blaquiere to improve yacht building in England, and, as a matter of fact, some eighty-five English yachts had their bows lengthened, or "Americanized," in the next two years.

Under British sailing the America was not so uniformly successful, probably because they did not trim her sails flat enough, and may be said to have had some unhappy years. She was sold to Lord Templeton who sank her by accident and then disposed of her to Messrs. Pritchard, ship builders on the Thames. The next heard of her, she was found scuttled in a Florida inlet where she had been attempting to run the blockade during the Civil War. She was raised and taken into the United States service, whereupon she began, as it were, to enjoy a less stormy life.

The cup won by the America in 1851, was in 1857 presented by the former owners of the yacht to the New York Yacht Club, and was open to challenge by any yacht club of any foreign country.

Another well known yacht of those days was the Silvie, owned by L. A. Depau. She received the first prize for schooners in a race around Long Island in 1858. She was taken to England and raced the English squadron, coming in second in spite of being becalmed.

Grand Military Steeplechase at London, Canada West,
May 9, 1843

The three-mile race at the Fashion Race Course, Long Island,
Saturday, June 21, 1856

[106]

HORSE RACING

1815-1860

ORSE racing between 1815 and the Civil War went through an epoch-making era with revolutionary developments.

Public races were prohibited in New York State in 1802, but the sport was continued in the Jockey Clubs. A prohibition in 1820 in Pennsylvania had the same result. But in 1821 New York permitted public racing in Queens County, which led to the founding of the New York Jockey Club in 1825, and the construction of the new Union Course on Long Island.

In 1816 Timoleon, by Sir Archy, a son of Diomed, set a new record by running a mile in 1:47, which held good for some years.

One of the most consistent winners was American Eclipse, by Duroc, out of a dam by Messinger. In 1822 he defeated James J. Harris's Sir Charles, of Virginia. This led to the most important race in America up to that time, — the one between American Eclipse, as representative of the North, and any Southern horse to be named, for $20,000.

Col. William R. Johnson of Petersburg, Virginia, offered to produce the horse from the South and in 1823 came north with several thorough-breds. His first choice, John Richards, was lamed, and he selected the four-year-old, Henry, or Sir Henry as he was often called.

John C. Stevens was the chief backer of American Eclipse, and the race was truly intersectional in character and importance.

On the morning of the race the road from New York to the Union Course on Long Island, a distance of eight miles, was covered with horse-men and a triple line of carriages. The stands were jammed, the clubhouse and the balcony filled with ladies, and the whole track lined on the inside by carriages and horsemen. There were estimated to be over 60,000 spectators at the course.

The first heat was won by Henry in the remarkably fast time of 7:37½ for the four miles. For the second heat, Eclipse, who needed to be urged and at the same time tightly reined, was ridden by Mr. Purdy, instead of the boy Crafts, who could not manage him. Toward the end of the heat, Purdy slipped Eclipse past Henry on the inside and won in 7:49. For the third heat Arthur Taylor replaced the boy Waldron on Henry, but Eclipse seemed to stand the distances better and won in 8:24.

At the Washington, D. C. Jockey Club, in 1834, was run perhaps the first of the rare early "hurdle races" of the country. There were six fences in the mile, and each gentleman rode his own horse, for plate valued at £100. At the last barrier, Mr. Stratton's horse leaped over one of the leading horses and the fence at one bound.

A genuine steeplechase, and the first in Canada, was run near Montreal in 1840. The course was circular and covered three miles of country, including three brooks and about twenty fences of rails or walls, four or five feet high. The grounds were crowded with carriages and horsemen. There were nine horses in line mostly belonging to army officers. Colonel Whyte on Heretic took the first leap and maintained the lead to the end. The delight of the beholders was so extreme that other steeplechases were predicted for the near future.

In 1836, thirteen years after Henry lost to Eclipse, Colonel William R. Johnson, of Petersburg, Virginia, got back at the North when in another South-versus-North race he selected John Bascombe, belonging to Colonel John Crowell of Alabama, and with him defeated Robert Tillotson's Post Boy in 7:49 and 7:51½ at the Union Course, Long Island. This race, like the previous intersectional contest, aroused the greatest interest both North and South and was discussed by the newspapers far and wide.

The third of these great intersectional races was for $20,000 and be-

Grand entrance to the Fashion Race Course, Long Island, 1856

Bird's-eye view of the Fashion Race Course, Long Island, 1856

tween truly representative champions of the North and South. The North depended upon Fashion, by Imported Trustee from a dam descended from Sir Archy. The South was represented by Boston, whose sire, Timoleon, had broken the mile record in 1816. Fashion was owned by Mr. William Gibbons of Madison, New Jersey; Boston belonged to Mr. Nathaniel Reeves of Richmond.

On May 20, 1842, when the race was run, the crowds seeking to get to the track were so great that thousands failed to find transportation, and the course was almost swamped with the flood of humanity.

The first heat showed tremendous bursts of speed by Fashion and remarkably consistent running by Boston. Both horses beat the record, Fashion winning in 7:32, the fastest time ever made in America. Fashion took the second heat also, but in slower time, 7:45.

In another North-and-South race in 1845, with $20,000 at stake, Fashion was defeated by Peytona, daughter of Glencoe, and entered by Thomas Kirkham of Alabama. The race was entered upon largely because Fashion had been beaten by Peytona in 1842, but the time 7:39¼ and 7:45¼ was slower than in the Fashion-Boston race.

Quarter racing at the county fairs was in the meantime falling into disrepute, not because it was not exciting but because it was open to too much trickery. An old quarter-mile racer could run on the drop of the hat, and was sometimes ridden from fair to fair looking for victims. Several humorous stories of quarter-miling in Kentucky indicate why it was condemned. At one fair the race was broached by a young fellow apparently in his cups who boasted of an old nag he had with him. Out of the crowd stepped seemingly a country yokel who took him up in behalf of an old horse he would produce. The betting went back and forth until it reached $500. Then the horses were produced and about the same time appeared a fat man and a tall man, both addressed as Colonel, who, it developed, were the owners of the horses. It also came out that the men who started the race talk were their matchmakers and bettors. Neither Colonel knew the other, but when the tall one saw the fat one's nag, he exclaimed, "Ha, if it isn't Old Starface!" And when the fat Colonel beheld the tall one's horse, he cried out, "Brown Imp, by gad!"

"Well, Colonel," said the fat one, " I didn't come down here to meet any horse like the Imp."

"Nor I any old timer like Starface," said the other.

"Gentlemen," said the fat one, "we don't want to put up any $500 on any little race like this. Let's call it off."

But the crowd, now all agog, wanted to see a race, and so the two old sharpers reduced the bet to small change, and the horses lived up to their reputations by running a hair-raising dead heat, whereupon all bets were declared off.

Curiously enough the time of the Fashion-Boston best heat was bettered but little until it was done at New Orleans by two sons of Boston, Lexington and Lecomte. After splitting races, Lecomte in 1854 defeated Lexington on the Metairie Course at New Orleans in the record time of 7:26, 7:38¾. The next year Lexington on the same course beat Lecomte's time and set a new record by making the four miles in 7:19¾, and then defeated Lecomte in 7:23¾, the fastest time in a race to that date.

Ripton and Confidence, Long Island, 1844

Trotting match on the Union Course, Long Island, 1851

TROTTING

1800–1860

WHILE running races were being carried on by the planters of the South and the jockey clubs of the North, a new type of horse racing was being developed in the North. In the South the planters still rode as a means of transportation, and rode to hounds as a recreation, but near the big cities of the North there was practically no foxhunting and comparatively little riding, either for transportation or pleasure. On the other hand driving was becoming fashionable. It had been a popular amusement in the winter and with sleighs for a century, and with the construction of light rigs, it began to be continued into the summer. At first the gait most in use was pacing, but the racking motion in harness was not especially pleasing to the driver, and attention was turned to the little known trotting.

The rise of trotting in the second quarter of the nineteenth century has all the elements of a drama. The gait was disliked abroad as not good for riding, and was not even favored for driving. Although we have noted previously that about 1770 horses in western Massachusetts were in some instances permitted to trot, the gait was not recognized on the race tracks. The greatest sire of all the trotters, Messenger, was brought over from England as a runner. Foaled in 1780 and winner of the King's Plate in 1785, Messenger was imported in 1788 by Mr. Benger of Pennsylvania. The passage was a rough one, and the tradition is that the other horses on the vessel were so weak that they had to be helped off the boat, but that Messenger charged down the gangplank with a neigh and that it took two grooms to hold him.

At first he was taken to Bristol, Pennsylvania, and then was purchased by Mr. Henry Astor and moved to Long Island. He was a grey, fifteen hands, three inches high, stoutly built, and upright at the shoulders. His trotting gait was not even noticed, because not put to use; but besides being the sire of such good runners as Potomac, Hambletonian, and Mambrino, from Mambrino and Hambletonian and from Messenger's grandson, Abdallah, came the greatest family of trotters. Of the fifty-two trotting stallions advertised in the *Spirit of the Times* in 1868, every one was descended from Messenger.

One of the few other trotting families of importance came from General De Lancey's True Briton, the horse previously mentioned, which he rode in the Revolution. He was the sire of Justin Morgan, foaled in 1793, from whom is traced the Morgan line. Justin Morgan was low, compact, and powerful, but with free action. His son, Fox, was driven 175 miles in twenty-four hours.

There are traditions that a horse called Yankee in 1806 trotted a mile, presumably under a saddle, on Harlem Lane in 2:59, and that in 1810 a horse from Boston went a mile at Philadelphia in 2:48½; but both distance and records were then rather carelessly measured.

The first known time that a horse ever trotted in public for a stake was in 1818. This was on a bet of $1,000 that was made at a jockey club dinner where the statement was proffered that no horse could be produced that could trot a mile in three minutes. The proposition was accepted by Major William Jones of Long Island and Colonel Bond of Maryland, but the betting was big odds on "time." The horse selected was Boston Blue, which won the bet by a narrow margin. He was purchased by Thomas Cooper, the tragedian, who used to drive him between New York and Philadelphia, to keep his theatrical engagements. Later Boston Blue was sent to England where he won a hundred sovereigns by trotting eight miles in 28:55, to beat half an hour.

The influence of Arabians in England led in 1820 to the importation of Grand Bashaw, among whose descendants was George M. Patchen.

In 1824 Albany Pony was reported to have trotted a mile in 2:40 on the straight-away turnpike at Jamaica.

The gait was becoming recognized as valuable for driving and in 1825 the New York Trotting Club was formed, which established a course on Long Island, probably the first especially for trotting.

One reason for this was that the speed of the descendants of Messenger was attracting attention, and there were recognized reliable lines to be followed in breeding. The Hunting Park Association for trotting was founded in Philadelphia in 1828.

One of the most remarkable trotting horses of that date was Top Gallant, by Hambletonian, foaled in 1808. He won his most important races when twenty years old, after trotting had taken its place on the track. He trotted four miles in 11:06; twelve miles in harness in 38:00, three miles under saddle in 8:31, and a mile in 2:45. Top Gallant was beaten by Betsey Baker, three miles in 8:16, who was in turn defeated by Screw Driver in 8:02 for the same distance.

Long races were common and indeed the trotters seemed to be expected to travel all day. Tom Thumb was taken over to England and in 1829 trotted 16½ miles in harness in 56:45, and 150 miles in nine hours and a half. In 1831 Chancellor trotted thirty-two miles against two hours and made the distance in one hour, 58 minutes, 31 seconds.

The mile record was broken in 1834 by Edwin Forrest, who trotted the distance in 2:31½, but he was afterward beaten in New England for a $10,000 stake by Daniel D. Tompkins.

The ancestry of one of the great trotting horses of that period, the Dutchman, was unknown, and he came to the tracks without prestige; but in 1839 on the Beacon Course in New Jersey he trotted three miles in 7:32½. Then came the era of Lady Suffolk, a granddaughter of Messenger, foaled in 1833, who was on the tracks until twenty years of age. She split races with the Dutchman, and in 1845 at the Beacon Course, first broke 2:30 by trotting a mile in 2:29½. She seemed to improve with the years, and in 1849 defeated Mac at Cambridge in 2:26.

Better known to-day, with a fame that has trickled down the years, is Flora Temple, granddaughter of Kentucky Hunter. In 1849 when four years old, she was sold for $13, and again for $68. She was taken to New York, where she began to earn repute on Harlem Lane, whence she was taken to the tracks. In 1852 she was sold for $4,000, and the next year she defeated Highland Maid in two great races. In 1854 she was bought by James McMann, who drove her even after he had sold her to William McDonald for $8,000. In a great race against Princess at Kalamazoo in 1859 she won the third heat in 2:19¾, putting the record below 2:20 for the first time. This feat was telegraphed throughout the nation and she became a public institution.

In her long career she helped greatly to create a flair for driving amongst the wealthy. A Wall Street man could step from his office or home into his light buggy behind his fast roadster and driving up Eighth Avenue or the Boulevard to Harlem Lane, could have a few brushes with other drivers and get his share of exercise, fresh air, and excitement.

Flora Temple's exhibitions and races did much to popularize trotting and establish it as an accepted feature of all state and county fairs, and indeed to keep racing from coming entirely under the legislative ban.

St. George Club match at their home grounds, 1844

Cricket match between the New England and St. George Clubs, 1851

BALL GAMES

1830-1860

WHILE by-laws for a cricket club at Boston have been unearthed dated as early as 1809, the game was never played widely throughout the country, but was kept alive if not very active at Boston, New York, and Philadelphia.

As early as 1840 we find the New York Cricket Club challenging the Toronto Cricket Club for $500 a side. At the match played at Toronto, the New Yorkers won, though not favored in the betting even in New York. The Torontos scored 52 in their first inning and 54 in their second; but New York won by 107 to 106 with no wickets down in their second inning.

This was the first of the international matches in which a team from the United States took part, and "created a good deal of excitement."

In 1844 the St. George's Club played a match at their home grounds against an All-Canada eleven for $1,000. The Canadians scored 82 runs in their first inning and 63 in their second, while the New York Club made 64 in their first inning, and scored 58 in their second without their best batter, who did not appear in time to take his turn. This match had run over from two days before, the second day's play being postponed on account of rain, and the delinquent one thought the grounds would still be too wet. As a result, the St. George's lost amid much excitement, and the tardy player was assailed by various cursory remarks when he arrived ten minutes too late.

The amounts of the wagers are significant, because these were supposed to be amateur clubs, whether the players were all amateurs or not.

The impression gathered from the sporting records of that era, is that while sport was less general than at present, there was then comparatively more betting in it than now. The conception of an amateur had not as yet crystalized for the guidance of either the individuals or the clubs.

In 1851 the St. George's Cricket Club played an important inter-sectional match against a cricket eleven of New England, and won at Cambridge with the need of only one inning.

It was perhaps unfortunate for cricket that it did not begin to take hold in the United States until the very era when baseball was beginning to develop. The earliest of the large cricket clubs near New York was the St. George's, founded in 1838, and the New York founded before 1840. The New England eleven was organized in 1850, and the Philadelphia Cricket Club in 1855. The oldest of the American cricket clubs still in existence is probably the Germantown Cricket Club, organized in 1855. The long-influential Young America Cricket Club was founded in Philadelphia later in the same year. The Manhattan Cricket Club dated its existence from 1856, and the Boston Cricket Club from 1857. All of these were important clubs, not only for cricket but socially, and most of them continued to be so for several decades. Cricket was a more leisurely game than baseball and was therefore more social in its nature. There might even be tea on the lawn, English fashion, and certainly there was more opportunity during an inning to chat with lady spectators. On the other hand, the games were not apt to be finished in a day, nor to be as close in the scores as baseball, nor as interesting to American spectators. As a consequence, while it might be just as good a game for the players, it was not as well adapted as baseball to draw crowds of onlookers who had only a few hours to spare. The greatest advantage of cricket over base-ball was its international popularity, which made it possible to stage games of comparatively great importance and patriotic interest.

In international matches played with Canada, the one at Harlem in 1853 was won by New York by 34 runs, while Canada won the match in 1854 in Toronto by 10 runs.

In 1856 an All-Canada Eleven played a United States Eleven from New York and Philadelphia at St. George's Cricket Club, losing by nine wickets. But in 1859 an All-England Eleven came over and at Hoboken defeated an All-United States twenty-two from New York and Philadelphia by the decisive score of 64 runs and an inning.

BASEBALL

Early in the nineteenth century ball games of various kinds were played by youngsters. One of the best known and most interesting was old cat. In one old cat there would be only one base besides home base, and perhaps only one or two batters who tried to get to and from the base on each hit. Or there might be more batters and more bases, when it was called two old cat or three old cat. Whenever a batter was put out, he went out into the field and everyone moved up a position.

One advantage of old cat was that it could be played by any number of players from four or five to a dozen. If there were more than this, sides could be chosen and runs counted for each side, when it began to approach baseball.

One form of this was town ball, which was played under rules in Philadelphia as early as 1833 by the Olympic Ball Club of that city. In this game, home was between two bases, balls knocked back of the batter counted as hits as in cricket, a runner hit with a thrown ball was out, and there were various other essential differences from baseball.

The first set of rules approximating those of baseball is probably that drawn up in 1839 by Abner Doubleday, who later became a brigadier general in the United States Army. While this introduced a diamond to inclose the bases, Doubleday allowed for eleven men on a side as in cricket.

In 1842 and 1843 a number of players used to meet for baseball at grounds on the site of the old Madison Square, 27th Street and Fourth Avenue. On propitious days two or three men would scout around in the

FOUR CENTURIES OF SPORT IN AMERICA

morning to get together enough players for a game. About 1844 they were driven from 27th Street to the north slope of Murray Hill, between Fourth and Third avenues.

In 1845 Alexander J. Cartwright proposed the organization of a club to be called the Knickerbocker Baseball Club. This was undertaken by himself; Duncan F. Curry, who became president; William R. Wheaton, elected vice-president; William H. Tucker, chosen secretary and treasurer; and E. R. Dupignac; the date of organization was September 23, 1845. In order to procure more permanent grounds, members of the club crossed the Hudson on the Barclay Street Ferry, and marched northward until they came to the Elysian Fields, Hoboken, where they set out their diamond.

To begin with, the games were played within the club. Two captains were selected, who chose sides. The rules provided that the side first making 21 runs won, that the ball must be pitched and not thrown, that the pitcher must be forty-five feet from home base, that a hit to be fair must pass between first and third base, that a batter was out who had three strikes or if his ball were struck or tipped or caught either on the fly or first bound; that the runner was out if the ball reached the base ahead of him or if he were touched with the ball, though it was not to be thrown at him; that three out put all out; that a runner interfering with a fielder was out, and that balks permitted him an advance of a base.

The Knickerbocker Baseball Club played its first outside game against a team picked from the other players around the city, called the New York team, and was beaten 23 to 1. As other baseball clubs began to organize, games were played against teams from them also. In 1851 the Knickerbocker twice defeated the Washington Club of Harlem, and the next year twice downed the New Gotham Club.

Other famous early clubs were the Eagle and the Empire of New York and the Excelsior of Brooklyn, all founded in 1854; the Union of Morrisania, and the Atlantic and the Eckford of Brooklyn, organized in 1855.

Cricket and baseball at Hoboken, 1859

Frank Pidgeon of the Eckfords told of the trepidation with which they entered upon their first outside game. They longed for a game with another club but were afraid to ask for it, dreading to be slaughtered. Finally they challenged the Union Base Ball Club of Morrisania, which accepted. Their friends wouldn't go to see them play, expecting a debacle, but the Eckford team won, 22 to 8 and returned home like peacocks with their tails spread.

In 1853 an All-New York nine defeated an All-Brooklyn team, two matches out of three, at the Fashion Race Course on Long Island.

Baseball was already being called the national game, as seen by the following passage from Porter's *Spirit of the Times*, 1856.

"With the fall of the leaf and the diminution of the daylight, many of the out-of-door sports and pastimes come to a close for the season. The manly and exhilarating pastimes of Base Ball, Cricket, Foot Ball, and Racket are not playable . . . We feel a degree of old Knickerbocker pride at the continued prevalence of Base Ball as the National game in the region of the Manhattanese."

The first volume of the new series of the *Spirit of the Times*, beginning in September, 1856, contained a number of notes on the games which were played after Thanksgiving day. In the December 6th issue, inundated by requests, the paper printed rules for the game. In these the bases were forty-two paces apart, the pitcher was fifteen paces from the batter, and twenty-one tallies made game.

Commenting on these rules, a correspondent wrote that in New England he had formerly played "round ball" with five bases, hits in any direction, and the pitcher throwing, not merely pitching, the ball.

A new set of rules was formulated by the New York clubs in February, 1857. One important movement toward amateurism was the rule that no player or umpire should bet on any game in which he took part.

In Philadelphia the first baseball clubs were the Minerva, organized in 1857, the Keystone of 1859, and the Athletic of 1860. Baseball was being played in the city square in Cleveland in 1857.

The National Association of Base Ball Players was organized in 1859. This was a strictly amateur association, just as all the clubs were as yet entirely amateur clubs. The clubs were still more or less social as well as athletic, just as the cricket clubs that began to be organized at about that time. Men who were interested in baseball joined a baseball club, and the club might have many times as many members as could ever hope to make the team of the club.

How little baseball was as yet standardized, may be inferred from the following account in *Harper's Weekly* accompanying an illustration of a game in 1859:

"Base-ball differs from cricket, especially, in there being no wickets. The bat is held high in the air. When the ball has been struck, the outs try to catch it, in which case the striker is out; or, if they cannot do this, to strike the striker with it when he is running, which likewise puts him out. Instead of wickets there are in this game four or five marks called bases, one of which, being the one at which the striker stands, is called home. As at cricket, the point is to make the most runs between these bases; the party which counts the most runs wins the day."

In stating that there might be five marks or bases, the writer apparently mixed up town ball and baseball, as they were both perhaps played on occasion by the players; and it is evident from his account that in some places the ball was still thrown at the runner who was out if he was hit.

FOOTBALL

Football, as it was first played in the United States, consisted of two sides comprising any number of players, kicking an inflated bladder or skin in a field toward two opposite goals any convenient distance apart. The ball had to be kicked and could not be carried or thrown. The constant rushes and efforts to kick the ball led to innumerable bruised shins, lamed legs, and crushed toes.

As early as 1829, the Sophomore and Freshman classes at Harvard fought for supremacy in a game of football on the first Monday of the fall term. It is significant of the roughness of the game that this day was known as Bloody Monday, but the interclass game was kept up year by year.

The game was played here and there in cities and colleges along the eastern seaboard, as late as the fifties having no special rules, except that the ball must be kicked.

Football was mentioned now and then in the *Spirit of the Times*, and an article in *Harper's Weekly* in 1857 is particularly striking, in contrast to the present complaints of over-emphasis in the colleges:

"The illustration which crowns these pages suggests another defect in our system. It is deficient in respect of physical training. That game of football, which we are happy to say is not yet extinct, ought to be a matter of as much concern as the Greek or mathematical prize. Indeed, of the two it is the more useful exercise. Here the English are vastly our superiors. . . . We had rather chronicle a great boat-race at Harvard or Yale, or a cricket match with the United States Eleven than all the prize poems or the orations on Lafayette that are produced in half a century."

Sophomore-Freshman football game at Harvard, 1857

OTHER SPORTS BEFORE THE CIVIL WAR

Sports for women in the United States before the Civil War were few, and were practiced only in the large cities or in special sections of the country, and only by exceptional women rather than by the majority.

In winter they enjoyed sleighing but the driving was almost always done by the men. Many more took part in skating, as may be seen from the prints of the period. The skates were still the old type with wooden tops and with blades that curved in a circle above the toe. Even on the ice many of the ladies took the air by being pushed about on miniature sleighs, although a fair number learned to skate well enough to strike out alone, or to time their strokes to those of a partner.

There was a revival of skating in New York City in 1859, as may be judged from an article in *Harper's Weekly*, which moreover speaks particularly of the part taken by the ladies in the sport:

"Never was there such a rage for skating throughout the United States as this winter. Before the age of steamboats, when the ice used to 'take' smoothly and broadly every Winter on the East and North Rivers, the New Yorkers were proverbially fond of skating. But for the last thirty years or so, the want of suitable ice has deprived the Gothamites of the pastime. This winter a bold and successful effort to repair the deficiency has been made by the Commissioners of the Central Park, who have turned their ponds and swamps to good use by flooding them every cold night, and inviting skaters to try them in the morning. The idea has been a hit. Thousands of persons of both sexes have for the past month, when-

ever the weather suited, spent an hour or two every day in the Park —
with no small advantage, it is to be hoped, to their health and spirits. . . .

"Throughout the North and East skating has long been a favorite
amusement with ladies as well as men. At Boston most of the young ladies
skate, and skate well. Throughout the Canadas skating rinks are a domes-
tic and popular institution. No doubt much of the health and fresh com-
plexion which distinguish Northern belles arise from this favorite pursuit."

In the summer a small number of the ladies rode horses or ponies and
drove their own rigs for amusement. There were riding academies in New
York and Boston where the fair ones were helped safely through their
first experiences on horseback. Indeed, the use of the side saddle made
preliminary training necessary. At the Massachusetts fair in Great Barrington, there was a ladies' race in which, it is important to note, the ladies
were judged not only from the speed of their horses, but more especially
from the grace and elegance of their riding.

Such equestrienne exhibits led to considerable discussion and letters
to the press on the subject. *The Spirit of the Times* commented on this
in part:

"A lot of cynical old fogies . . . have recently been startled . . . by
the rushing, galloping, slashing, and dashing exploits of the lady eques-
trians at the agricultural fairs. This jocund spectacle like everything else
that is new . . . does not suit the still veins of these respectable old goats.
. . . But still the ladies go on riding. . . ."

The custom spread rapidly for a time and ladies' riding exhibits became quite a regular attraction at the fairs. Some of the lady riders even
went so far as to challenge others whom they "had heard to be skilful
riders" to such a contest.

In the South, young ladies rode much more generally than in the
North, at least in certain sections. Note the following extract from a letter
of 1856, for example:

"We once approached an old Virginia farmhouse, with its owner who
had been for some days absent. A few hundred yards off, we suddenly

Ten-mile foot race at Hoboken in 1845

Ladies' race at the fair of the Housatonic Agricultural Society,
Great Barrington, Mass., 1857

[133]

The tenpin player, 1842

The billiard player, 1842

stopped to gaze, for, at that moment, dashing round from the rear of the mansion, and darting like mad through the trees, came a troop of riders at full speed, all of them females but one."

The youngest rider was a mere child of twelve, who reined her horse on its haunches to avoid a closing gate.

"Our boys and girls can never rest with trotting a horse for a mile," remarked the owner of the plantation, comparing customs there with those farther north.

But even in the South, though the men rode regularly, the women certainly rode only occasionally, possibly because the carriage with its negro coachman was so omnipresent.

Archery was practiced in Philadelphia and in a very few other places, but its revival as a social exercise did not come until a few years later. Croquet, which was introduced into England from France in 1856, was scarcely known in the United States in 1860, though it was played here soon afterward, in the time of the Civil War.

The ladies enjoyed boating, and while an exceptional one liked to take a hand at the oars or a paddle, the greater number preferred a parasol in the stern seat, to strenuous efforts and blisters on the palms.

A very few in the rare mansions that had a billiard table, might now and then take up a cue, but they were admittedly the veriest tyros whose attempts were not considered serious even by themselves.

We read, in the *Spirit of the Times* in 1856, of young matrons taking a stand in a deer drive in the Adirondacks; in this particular case the deer was shot at another stand not far distant. Other rare notices prove that a few ladies, even in the East, had learned to handle a gun.

Walking and running races began to get public notice in the first volumes of the *American Turf Register*. In the winter of 1830-31, in Philadelphia, Joshua Newsam walked one thousand miles in eighteen days. In 1835 there was a great foot race at the Union Course on Long Island. The distance was ten miles, and the purse $1,000 with a special prize added for bettering an hour. Henry Stannard of Killingworth won the match, making the first mile in 5:36, the last mile in 5:54, and the ten miles in 59:44.

The fact that Stannard covered ten miles in less than an hour, created a wide interest and gave good round figures to run against.

In 1844 these races received an international flavor when Thomas Greenhalgh and John Barlow came over from England to contest at the Beacon Course, Hoboken. At one race the crowd of 25,000 broke into the grounds and was with difficulty kept under control sufficiently to let the race go on. This race, which was for $1,000, was won by John Gildersleeve, a chair gilder of New York, who ran the ten miles in 57:01½, with Thomas Greenhalgh second, and John Barlow third. Another ten-mile race was won by John Barlow of England, who covered the distance in the faster time of 54:21, with John Steeprock, the Indian, second, and Greenhalgh and Gildersleeve following. At the end of the year a twelve-mile race was won by Greenhalgh in 68:48.

These races attracted so much interest that a boatload of four hundred spectators came down to one race from Albany, and the *Illustrated London News* printed a woodcut of another. The contestants were all professionals or anxious to be such, and the contests in this form seem never to have been taken up by amateurs in the United States, but this did not lessen the interest of the spectators as long as there was no question that each man was doing his best.

Although billiards was played in practically all the best clubs and in many mansions where the owner had a flair for it, we learn from an article in the *New York Atlas* in 1841, that sharpers were besmirching the game in the hotels and public billiard rooms. Billiards, in fact, was in much the same position as court tennis in England a century earlier. It was so entirely a game of skill that a professional could gauge an amateur's game to a nicety and make it appear in every game as if his opponent, with a little luck, might have won.

Some of the professionals took advantage of this to lead on the innocents in public halls and hotels, and some of them even went so far as to

The great billiard match between M. Phelan and J. Seereiter
at the Fireman's Hall, Detroit, 1859

*The great prize fight between Morrissey and the Binecia Boy
at Long Point, Canada West, 1858*

[138]

dress themselves like small town boys in the hopes of more easily luring on the victims.

About 1850, however, Michael J. Phelan published his book emphasizing the science of the game, and as professional champion did much to put it in higher popular repute. At that time billiards was played in English style with four balls on a six by twelve-foot table, which had pockets at all four corners and at the sides. It was thus somewhat of an unseparated mixture of pool and billiards as they are now played in the United States. In 1857 Phelan visited Ireland and gave exhibitions for the benefit of the needy. In 1859 he played a championship match against John Seereiter, which aroused wide public attention, and on which it was said there was half a million in wagers. The match was played in Fireman's Hall at Detroit and lasted from about 7:30 p.m. until 5 a.m. Seereiter made the highest run, 157, but Phelan came close to it with 150. Phelan was slightly ahead for the most of the way, and finally won by 96 points.

While prize fighting had been carried on in the United States for many years, it had been against the law, and had been brought off under cover in the most disreputable surroundings. James "Yankee" Sullivan claimed the championship about 1841, then was beaten by Tom Hyer in 1849. But prize fighting scarcely came into national prominence until the time of John Morrissey, who won the championship by defeating Hyer in 1853.

In 1858 he was challenged by John C. Heenan, who like Morrissey was of Irish descent but born in this country. In order to meet they went to Buffalo, where two boats were secured which carried them to Long Point, Canada, about ninety miles distant. The fight was with bare fists under the old London Prize Ring rules, which allowed wrestling and holding in chancery, and continued each round until one man was on the ground. A second rope was stretched twenty feet outside the ring to keep the crowd away, and there were fifty ring keepers, including "Dad Cunningham, who had recently killed Paudeen."

The battle was a desperate one, and when it was seen that Heenan could not come up for the twelfth round, his crowd broke into the ring and stopped the fight. Morrissey claimed the victory, and, it may be added, later became a member of Congress from the 5th New York District.

Two years later Heenan went over to England to fight Tom Sayers, who held the championship belt there. The fight was against the law, and Heenan was bound over to keep the peace, but this was a mere form and the battle came off. This was another vicious fight. Sayers drew the first blood but Heenan got first throw and first knockdown. From the thirty-eighth round on, Sayers' backers tried to break up the fight, and at the beginning of the forty-second round, when Sayers could not come to the mark, his adherents rushed the ring and stopped the battle. Heenan was presented with a duplicate championship belt, and the fracas led to the formulating of a new set of rules by the Marquis of Queensbury.

THE CIVIL WAR DECADE

WHILE the college regattas were dropped for several of the Civil War years, and the other regattas diminished in numbers and importance, they did not cease entirely.

In 1860 in the Second College Union Regatta, class raced class for the first time, the Harvard Freshman and Sophomore crews defeating the Yale class crews. Then the championship boats of Harvard, Yale, and Brown raced one another, Harvard winning, with Yale second. This was the last of the college regattas for four years.

But in the meantime, the professional oarsmen were keeping in the public eye. At the Boston Regatta in 1862, James Hamill of Pittsburgh, came in so far ahead that the judges refused to salute him as the winner, thinking he had covered only part of the course. They saluted the second man, Doyle, as victor, much to his astonishment, but he promptly assured them that Hamill had rowed over all of the course.

In August, 1862, Hamill challenged Joshua Ward, who held the championship belt and was considered the best oarsman in America. Hamill won two matches against Ward that year, but in July, 1863, Ward in turn beat him at Poughkeepsie. This led in September to a big championship contest for $2,000 at Poughkeepsie, which Hamill won after a struggle in fast time. Later Hamill went to England to row Kelley, the English champion, but was defeated in two challenges.

In 1865 there was a widely heralded match for $5,000 at Poughkeepsie between two four-oared boats, the Floyd T. F. Field of that city and the Samuel Collyer of New York. The local boat had the cheers of the whole town, which turned out to see the race, but the New York boat won.

In the College Union Regatta, which was renewed in 1864, the Yale boat won for the first time and repeated the next year, but Harvard then had a streak of five straight victories.

In 1869 Harvard challenged Oxford for a match which took place on the Thames River in August, 1869. This was the first of the international rowing contests and excited the greatest interest both in England and America. On the day of the match London was deserted, the river was lined with a hundred thousand spectators, the bridges crowded.

The boats were sent off by the mere words, "Off, gentlemen," from the starter. Harvard rowed high stroke, about 43, while Oxford's stroke was several counts lower. Harvard started off ahead and at a mile and a half had gained a lead of about two lengths. But from this point, the Harvard crew was not able to keep up its speed, and Oxford, rowing steadily and strongly, gradually cut down the lead and won the race.

In 1860 the yacht Julia, built by George Stern and owned by John Waterbury, defeated the Rebecca, owned by James G. Bennett, Jr., on a course twenty miles to the windward of Sandy Hook and return. But the war was coming on, and with its advent many of the yachts were taken into government service, and there was very little yacht racing of importance until after the conflict.

In 1865 began a series of sporting races between well known yachts of prominent yachtsmen. The Fleetwing, owned by G. A. Osgood, defeated the Henrietta, owned by James G. Bennett, Jr., from Sandy Hook to Cape May. Then the Henrietta recovered some of her prestige by defeating the N. B. Palmer over the same course. The next year E. Osgood came forward with the Widgeon and by the aid of its time allowance defeated Pierre Lorillard's Vesta for a $1,000 wager, over a course from Newport to Block Island and return. The Vesta thereupon tangled up all claims to the championship by defeating the Henrietta on a $1,000 bet, in a gale of wind from Sandy Hook to Cape May and back.

This led to the famous transatlantic yacht race of the Fleetwing, Vesta, and Henrietta. The owners of the Fleetwing and Vesta first bet $30,000 on their two boats, then the Henrietta was let into the race by also putting up $30,000. The race was the big feature of the time and was discussed all over the nation and in England and on the Continent.

The start was made December 11, 1866, and the passage was rough. The Fleetwing had the tragic misfortune of having four men swept overboard and lost while furling the jib. Two others were saved with difficulty. The race was won by the Henrietta, which had been having rather the worst of the local contests, but now made good all claims to seaworthiness and speed. The time was 13 days and 22 hours, which was fast for sailing.

Just before the Civil War, Flora Temple was still Queen of the trotting tracks. In 1860 she had beaten George M. Patchen six times in hard races and five times in special matches at one and two miles. The next year she defeated John Morgan, of the well known Morgan family of trotters, three times in matches at one, two, and three miles. Then came the war, and she went into honored retirement.

Trotting was kept up but in a local and smaller way. A new track was opened in 1862 in New York between Seventh and Eighth avenues at 144th Street, and the *Spirit of the Times* continued to carry reports of trotting races, the purses being small and the horses little known.

After the war, however, trotting started to boom. The leaders among the trotters were Dexter, Lady Thorn, American Girl, and Goldsmith Maid, and they were so closely matched for two or three years that a blanket could be spread over the lot. In 1867 Dexter, who was by Rysdyk's Hambletonian, made 2:19 in a race and 2:17 against time, whereupon he was purchased by Robert Bonner of New York and reserved for private driving.

Robert Bonner was the nationally known publisher of the *New York Ledger*. He had begun driving for his own amusement and started a stable in 1856. This had remained undeveloped during the war, but after peace was declared, Bonner became the greatest supporter of strictly amateur driving. He purchased, one after another, several of the horses that lowered the world's trotting record.

Lady Thorn was rather the best of the big campaigners in the fall of 1868, and had trotted a mile under 2:19; but in June, 1869, American Girl defeated Lady Thorn, Lucy, and Goldsmith Maid in three straight heats, the second at 2:19. American Girl's dam had been bought for $40 by White Travis in Virginia at the opening of the war to help him get back North. Her sire was Cassius M. Clay, Jr., and she was foaled in 1862. When five years old she was brought to the speedways in New York, whence she was soon taken to the tracks. In 1869 she defeated Goldsmith Maid four times, but on August 11th, Goldsmith Maid came into her own in the greatest race of that era.

Goldsmith Maid was by Edsall's Hambletonian, later called Alexander's Abdallah, and was foaled in 1857. As a filly she was very high strung and was sold to Alden Goldsmith for $650. He treated her very gently, never touching her with a whip, and eventually got her to be easily managed and dependable. In 1868 she was sold to B. Jackman and the famous driver, Budd Doble, for $20,000.

At the Buffalo Driving Park, August 11, 1869, for a $10,000 purse, and with 20,000 spectators cheering on the famous mares, Goldsmith Maid defeated American Girl and Palmer in three amazing heats, every one of which was trotted below 2:20. In the third heat American Girl led Goldsmith Maid at the half-mile by three lengths, but Goldsmith Maid outlasted her and won out. The timing was 2:19¾, 2:19½ and 2:19¾, which constituted the fastest average and most consistent record-breaking time made up to that date. This record was telegraphed around the country, and it began to be definitely acknowledged that the below-2:20 era had arrived. This race seemed to give Goldsmith Maid the edge over American Girl, whom she defeated five times afterwards that year. Two years later she broke Dexter's record against time and afterwards lowered her own record to 2:14.

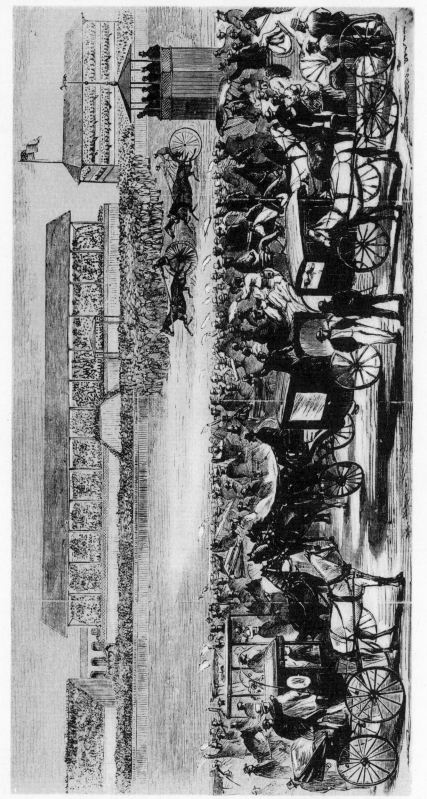

Goldsmith Maid defeating American Girl at the Buffalo Driving Park, 1869

[145]

Largely due to Robert Bonner's influence, the Driving Club of New York was founded in 1869, and did much to create the era of the fancy driving horse that followed.

Because running races had been more popular in the South than in the North, they were interfered with more by the war than was trotting. But in 1864 William R. Travers and John Hunter inaugurated a new course at Saratoga, a year after racing was established at Paterson.

In this whole post-war epoch the outstanding horse in the East was Kentucky, sired by Lexington and foaled in 1861 from a dam by Glencoe. At Paterson in 1864, he defeated Aldebaran, by Commodore, and at Saratoga won the Travers Stakes for three-year-olds.

The next year Kentucky won the Saratoga Cup and dominated the course. This was the first highly fashionable meeting since before the war and was so inspiring that *Harper's Weekly* wrote of it:

"The second annual meeting of the Saratoga Association was the occasion of a series of horse races the most splendid ever witnessed on this continent. . .

"Imagine 1200 persons seated at dinner at the Union Hotel, a thousand at Congress Hall. . .

"We shall not attempt to discuss the triumphs of that magnificent horse Kentucky, nor of his extraordinary companions in glory. . ."

Kentucky won the Saratoga Cup in 1866 and from there was taken to New York for the opening of the new Jerome Park. This was called by *Turf*, *Field*, *and Farm* "the greatest event in the history of the turf in America."

"Here at Jerome Park," continued this paper, "we have a few private individuals who manfully come to the front and with princely liberality expend enormous sums for the benefit of their fellow countrymen and to establish an institution that will be a perpetual benefit and place of amusement to future generations."

All of which to-day sounds like a rather wild prophecy.

Jerome Park was opened by the American Jockey Club, which was founded by Leonard W. Jerome, W. R. Travers, and August Belmont. In the Inauguration Stakes, Kentucky defeated Fleetwing, Onward, and others, four miles in 7:35 and 7:41½. The next year Kentucky was purchased by Leonard W. Jerome, and, after a losing race against 7:20, retired.

In the meantime Asteroid at St. Louis, and Norfolk on the West Coast, both sired by Lexington, were regularly victorious, but they did not attain to the national reputation of Kentucky. In 1865 Leamington was imported from England and in a few years his descendants began to come into prominence. Tracks were built at Long Branch and other places, and racing seemed to be once more in full swing.

While the baseball and cricket clubs were pretty well depleted during the war, games continued to be reported regularly in the *Spirit of the Times*, though the cricket games were no longer international, and the baseball games were not so expertly played.

A little baseball was played in the army. Christmas Day, 1862, for example, at Hilton Head, South Carolina, Duryea's Zouaves' team played a picked nine from the other regiments. Accounts of baseball were passed on by soldiers from localities where it was played to those who knew nothing of it.

In the colleges baseball began to be played by class clubs, and in October, 1864, the Harvard Base Ball Club was organized from such class clubs. In each case the club seems to have been more than a team, and, in fact, made up of all those sufficiently interested in the game to join. In 1865 the Harvard Base Ball Club defeated one from Williams, 36-30. Then by beating a number of the town clubs won the unofficial championship of New England.

Right after the war baseball was taken up again with a rush. The convention of the National Association of Base Ball Players in 1865 had 91 clubs represented; in 1867 there were 237 clubs. Arthur Pue Gorman, later senator from Maryland, was made president in 1866.

Internal troubles began to develop, when the popularity of the game became so great that gate receipts became possible at the more noted contests. This led in 1865 to attempts by one club to get players to change to it from another club, which was forbidden by the association of players in New York but was hard to stop.

The increase in the crowds produced other consequences. In 1866, when the Atlantics of Brooklyn played the Athletics of Philadelphia for the unofficial championship of America, the crowd broke into the grounds at Philadelphia. The game was moved to the Capitoline grounds on Long Island, where "police protection was better." The Atlantics won 27 to 17 and were acknowledged the best team of the year.

In 1867 the National Base Ball Club of Washington, a team of amateurs, made a trip west, paying their own expenses, and won all their games but the one against the Forest Citys of Rockford, Illinois, for whom A. G. Spalding, then a youth of seventeen, pitched.

The direct monetary returns from a winning team, as well as the valuable publicity for a town, led to a demand for the best players and to payment for their services. The Excelsiors of Chicago had a semi-professional team as early as 1867, and Cincinnati had one the next year. In 1869 the Cincinnati Red Stockings were openly professionals, paid for all of their time, and in trips both east and to California won all their games. This initiated the era of professional baseball.

The development of professionalism clashed with the old idea of the club. Whereas the club had formerly been made up of practically anyone who wished to join because he liked to play, the professional team was picked for results and reduced to the smallest effective number. Curiously enough, the amateur term "club" has been handed down, though it is no longer applicable to the professional team.

The football game at the beginning of the fall term between the Harvard Sophomore and the Freshman classes, which had fastened the term "Bloody Monday" to the day, was prohibited by the college authorities in 1860 because of its brutality. Interclass games were also banned at Yale for the same reason.

But football was being played to some extent and by lesser groups at Harvard, Yale, Princeton, Rutgers, and a dozen colleges along the eastern seaboard.

In the war football was occasionally played in a small way as a recreation by the soldiers. A plate in *Leslie's Weekly* on army festivities in 1861 includes a sketch of soldiers chasing a football.

The game was still in general undeveloped "Association Football," with two crowds kicking the ball toward opposite goals and getting into dangerous mix-ups in seeking to get a chance to do so.

The first intercollegiate game was in 1869 when Princeton and Rutgers agreed to lay aside their feud over Revolutionary cannon in favor of a series of three football games. There were twenty-five on a side, the Princetonians trying to make goals with long kicks, the Rutgers team kicking short to one another and dribbling the ball in the effort to keep it in their possession.

Rutgers won the first game and Princeton the second. Of these the *New York Daily Tribune* printed the following:

"FOOT BALL

"This old English game is rapidly coming into favor in America. . . . In this country, the college students have taken to it this year with a fervor hitherto unknown. A second contest between Rutgers and Princeton Colleges was played last Saturday at Princeton, twenty-five on a side, and the victory fell to the latter, after eight successive games, Rutgers winning none. A third and final contest has been set down for to-day, which is to decide the series, Rutgers having been victorious in the first encounter two weeks ago."

But the third game threatened to develop into such a riot that it was stopped by the college authorities.

Fully as significant as the first intercollegiate game is the fact that there were calls upon the *Spirit of the Times* for information in regard to Rugby football, from which our present game is descended. This had been started at Rugby in 1820 by a student, William Webb Ellis, who introduced the idea of running with the ball, instead of kicking it. It was played there for decades, but not developed until about 1862. The news of the new game then spread rapidly, and in November, 1869, the *Spirit of the Times* printed the Rugby rules for the guidance of American inquirers.

Walking received a great deal of notice when Edward P. Weston, in the spring of 1861, walked from Boston to Washington, 478 miles, in ten days, as payment of a wager he had lost in betting against Lincoln. This gave him considerable publicity, and his feat was used to indicate the distances possible to troops under forced marches in the war.

In 1861 Deerfoot, the Seneca Indian, was taken to England, and, after losing a race or so before he got into condition, beat all the English runners at about ten miles, or in an hour's time, in race after race. He ran in breechclout and moccasins, with a feather in his hair, and became a great sensation, his races attracting the presence of members of the royal family and of the greatest crowds that had ever attended running races there.

Weston in 1867 won $10,000 by walking from Portland, Maine, to Chicago in twenty-six days. He became a national figure, and almost alone established an epoch of long-distance walking in this country.

In England, Charles Kingsley's demand for a muscular instead of an ascetic Christianity did a great deal toward encouraging "manly exercises," as they were once called. This gradually led to the introduction into clubs of athletics which for the English and Americans took the place of the gymnastic exercises in the German turnerbund. The important New York Athletic Club was founded in 1868, holding a little indoor athletic meeting in a skating rink that year and an outdoor meeting the next year in Central Park.

Both speed skating and fancy skating were being developed. There were local races between skaters in the time of the war, though no attempt was made to evolve a national champion.

In fancy skating, Jackson Haines was supreme and, moreover, revolutionized the art. He developed the many fancy movements and figures to a science and grace never before known. In 1864 he went to Europe where he influenced skating even more than in America, and, in fact, created a system there. When he died, a monument was erected to his skill and his memory became a legend.

In local New York in 1866, *Leslie's Weekly* said that Mr. Engler and Miss Henrietta Bedell were the best, "Mr. Engler going in any direction with equal facility," and illustrated "these two champions performing the backward roll on the outside edge of the skates," on the Union Pond in Williamsburg, New York.

An American skating congress was held in Pittsburgh in 1868 to encourage and regulate the sport.

Ice boats were coming in for use on the wide stretches of the Hudson and on small lakes near cities. *Harper's Weekly*, in 1869 wrote of them as follows:

"The ice-yacht is a boat on skates and is impelled by the wind in the same manner as an ordinary yacht. There has been for some time at Poughkeepsie, in this state, an Ice Boat Club. . . . With a strong wind and upon a smooth surface of ice, one of these ice boats will attain a speed of one mile a minute, thus outrunning the locomotive, and literally flying with the speed of the wind."

Other ice sports included curling, which was not common but was becoming known, and shinny, which had the elements of hockey but had not yet developed into it.

Bobsleds were in use, and tobogganing was one of the sports of Canada, but while written of in American periodicals was scarcely practiced here.

One little known game that staged a genuine international championship was racquets.

The New York Racquet Club, made up of "gentlemen of the highest standing," had built courts at 55 West 13th Street in 1863 and engaged Frederick Foulkes of England as professional. He was the best player in

Shooting wild pigeons in Iowa, 1867

Prairie-chicken shooting in Kansas, 1867

[153]

Victory of ice boats over the Chicago express train from New York,
near Poughkeepsie, N. Y., 1871

the United States, and in 1867 a home and home match was made between him and William Gray, the champion of Great Britain and Ireland, for £500.

The courts in New York, where the first match was played, were strictly first-class as then considered. The walls were of red brick, "even as ice," and the floor of the same material, but with good footing. The courts were well lighted and ventilated by windows, but the two galleries, as is usually the case with racquets and squash, were utterly inadequate to hold the crowd that wanted to watch the match. Gray won four out of seven games, and later in England completed his victory.

Billiards was interfered with by the war less than most other pastimes. For one reason it required only two to play it; for another it was on the crest of a fashionable wave due in part to a wider understanding of the scientific beauties of the game. There was a column on billiards in *Leslie's Weekly*, which helped to give it vogue in new circles. This was written by Michael Phelan, who was the great promoter of the game in this country.

Phelan by 1863 was becoming engrossed in the manufacture of the paraphernalia for the game and no longer cared to maintain his claim to the championship. Therefore in June, 1863, he helped to promote a tournament of professional players for the championship, the prize being a Phelan and Collender billiard table. This was played at Irving Hall before enthusiastic crowds, and won by Dudley Kavanagh, who thereupon became champion. At the end of the tournament a match was played between eastern and western teams, which was won by the East.

The game in America was rapidly improving, and the best players were leaving out the pockets, playing only caroms.

Kavanagh, because of sickness, defaulted in 1865 to Louis Fox, who was defeated by John Deery. In 1866, in the ninth championship match since 1863, held at Cooper Institute before a large crowd, Deery decisively defeated John McDevitt in an American carom game for 1500 points. Billiards had caught the popular attention and big matches were considered important enough to be illustrated in the press.

[155]

An indoor winter game, often associated in habitat with billiards, was bowling. Bowling on the green was done of old, but the indoor alleys were probably first developed in America.

When the Prince of Wales visited America in 1860, he tried bowling at Niagara Falls, as thus described in *Leslie's Weekly:*

"At the Falls he doffed his coat and went seriously to work at that peculiar American and decidedly healthy and invigorating game. He seemed to enjoy it very much and was tolerably successful in his maiden efforts at bowling."

Bowling was taken up by the Germans and, we suspect, encouraged by some of the growing breweries as an inciter to a healthy thirst, and by the end of the decade had become pretty well established.

Rifle shooting was logically encouraged by the war. In September, 1861, was held the fifth meeting of the National Rifle Club at Troy, which was won by L. Lewis. There had been turkey shoots and other such meetings for decades, and there had been German shooting societies in 1842, but the war gave an impetus to shooting at a target for the definite measurement and improvement of skill rather than merely to bag a prize. The sharpshooters of the war gathered a romance about them and inspired emulation amid less dangerous surroundings.

After the war an article appeared in the *Army and Navy Journal* in regard to rifle shooting, urging its encouragement, which led to the formation of the National Rifle Association in 1871.

To take the place of pigeon shooting, a spring trap which projected glass balls was developed about 1866, and soon came into general use for that purpose. This gave practice in shooting on the fly and came into favor with sporting clubs formed for fowling with shotguns rather than for target shooting with rifles.

The war was followed by a renewed and greatly increased interest in the shooting of game. Thousands of men had handled firearms in the war, who had not been accustomed to them before, and after peace came many of them applied their recently acquired skill to shooting for sport.

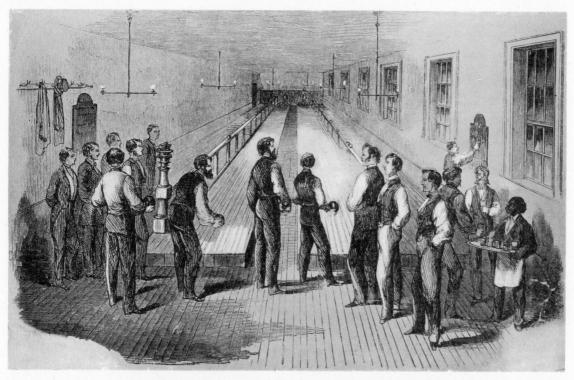

The Prince of Wales and his companions playing tenpins at Niagara, 1860

Croquet, 1866

[157]

A good evidence that field sports had begun to be accepted by the public conscience and were considered of widespread interest, is that sporting pictures, unemphasized by any particular event, began to appear in such national periodicals as *Harper's* and *Leslie's*. In 1866 *Leslie's Weekly* described the canvasback ducks on the Chesapeake, — how they dove for the roots of the wild celery, how the widgeons would try to steal it from them, and how they were shot from blinds. The shores there had already passed into possession of sportsmen and, according to the article, tolling the ducks and sailing upon them with a blunderbuss in the prow were no longer permitted.

In 1867 *Harper's Weekly* printed a picture of shooting prairie chickens from horses in Kansas. Dogs in advance of the party marked the game. This was flushed by the horses, which were well broken to permit the sportsmen to shoot from their backs without having a hand on the bridle. The chickens when shot were gathered by the dogs and were tied to the saddle. In the same periodical that year were woodcuts of squirrel shooting and raccoon hunting, which tends to measure the interest in these sports.

The great flights of the passenger pigeon were not yet over, and in 1867 *Leslie's Weekly* described one in Iowa. The pigeons arrived in vast flocks that darkened the air. Migrating a long distance from the South, they were individually half-starved and frantic for food, and as a mass frightfully destructive. They lit on the fields of new-sown grain, the masses behind the front line rolling over it again and again like the waves of the sea and cleaning up every kernel in their path. They covered forty acres at a time, and thousands of acres had to be sown over and harrowed in very deeply.

The next year, 1868, *Harper's Weekly* depicted grouse shooting, and deer hunting in the Adirondacks, both practiced within a short distance of New York City.

To a lesser extent fishing was also brought to the attention of the general public. Fishing for pickerel, and fishing in the Mississippi, off the coast of New Jersey, and in the Hudson, all were delineated as subjects of popular interest.

A new sport that was introduced in this era was velocipeding. There had been the old draisine, named after its inventor, Baron von Draisine, which was pushed by the feet, but in 1855 M. Michaux had brought out a velocipede with pedals. In 1865 Pierre Lallement had made the pedals turn on the cranks, which obviated their turning under the feet. Three years later, following the fashion in Paris, velocipeding became a mania here. It was pictured seriously in the periodicals, and caricatured gleefully in the same papers. Velocipede schools were established where men and women, young, middle-aged, and elderly, were taught to ride. A very important feature of it was that women could ride, which added a little to the few outdoor sports in which they took part.

A new outdoor game particularly adapted to women was croquet. While this was introduced into England only in 1856, it must have been brought into this country early in the war era. Louisa M. Alcott in *Little Women*, which novelized many of her own memories of the Civil War period, described a game of croquet between two sides chosen from a party of boys and girls.

Harper's Weekly in 1866 carried a picture of croquet, and described it as the greatest outdoor game for women yet invented. It required skill but not necessarily scientific technique, and not too much strength or activity for a lady. Moreover its courting and matchmaking qualities were considered beyond all praise.

The race for the America's Cup, 1870

Boating on the Harlem River in 1879

[162]

IN THE SEVENTIES

THE first big sporting event of the seventies was an international yacht race for the Royal Yacht Squadron Cup, won by the America in 1851. When this cup was deeded to the New York Yacht Club in 1857, notice was sent out to all foreign yacht clubs that it was open to challenge, but the war came on and the first race for it was not until 1870.

The challenge was issued in 1869 by James Ashbury of London, a member of the Royal Yacht Club, for his yacht Cambria. He had originally suggested that a defending yacht be sent to England, sail against the Royal Yacht Squadron there, race his yacht across the Atlantic, and sail against his yacht in American waters. This proposal had not been accepted by the New York Yacht Club, but William Bennett, vice-commodore of the club, took his yacht Dauntless across the ocean, and made the return voyage a transatlantic race against the Cambria. This was in every way a great race, and at the time was considered fully as important as the coming contest for the cup.

Mr. Bennett's Dauntless suffered the same tragic accident that had met the Fleetwing in the transatlantic race against his Henrietta the year before. In furling the jib in a gale, two men were swept overboard and lost in spite of diligent search. The Cambria won the race, but only by an hour and forty minutes, after a sail of 23 days, 5 hours, and 15 minutes.

Inasmuch as the Cambria had beaten the Dauntless, which was known to be one of the fastest yachts of the New York Yacht Club, she was considered a dangerous contender.

The race, like the one won by the America, included the yachts of the fleet, twenty-three in number. The America, now owned by the government, was in it. Of the contest *Harper's Weekly* said:

"The race was the most exciting one ever witnessed in American waters. The bay was covered with steamers and sailing vessels of every description, and it is estimated that the contest was witnessed by over a hundred thousand people, whose interest was heightened by the fact that among the contestants for the prize were the celebrated yacht America, the winner of the International yacht race of 1851, and the Cambria, which has just won the ocean race with the Dauntless. The Magic, one of the handsomest as well as one of the fastest yachts in the world, made the race in about three hours and fifty-eight minutes."

The Magic at the finish was followed by the Dauntless; then came the Idler and close behind her the America. The challenger, the Cambria, was eighth on corrected time, but it was nevertheless a great yacht race.

The Magic was a shoal, centerboard schooner of only 90 tons; the Cambria a schooner of 248 tons, with a keel, and a draft of twelve feet.

This contest, in direct results, was as influential as the original winning of the cup by the America, as it initiated the series of international races here.

But the sailing of a whole fleet against a lone challenger was admittedly not equitable, and when, after much correspondence, Mr. Ashbury again challenged for a series of four out of seven races the next year, the New York Yacht Club agreed to enter only one yacht against the challenger each day, though it reserved the right to pick any one of four for that race.

For the first race, which was over the club course, Commodore Osgood's Columbia was selected to oppose the Livonia and won by 27 minutes. For the second day it was thought that the Dauntless might be selected, as the course was twenty miles to windward and the wind fresh, but the Columbia was again chosen and led by 10 minutes. In the third race, however, the Columbia was disabled, and the Livonia won by a quarter of an hour. Then the New York Yacht Club turned to the Sappho, which was successful in the last two races.

The hulls of the American and English yachts were of entirely different types, and the victory of the American yachts was thought to confirm the superiority of their configuration, as *Harper's Weekly* declared:

"The possession of the cup is not the only question decided by the race. There is an essential difference in the principles of construction adopted by the yacht builders of England and America, and this contest has proved the superiority of the American mode. The English yachts are narrow and of deep draught, stiffness in heavy weather being secured by means of ballast — so much dead weight to be dragged through the water. American yachts, on the contrary, secure steadiness by great breadth of beam, which by causing them to sink less deep, insures far greater buoyancy without loss of stiffness. The English have always claimed that their yachts were more easily handled than the American, especially in heavy weather, but this race in which the American principle of construction was fairly matched against the English, has demonstrated the fallacy of that opinion."

The next challenge came from the Royal Canadian Yacht Club of Toronto, which sent down the Countess of Dufferin. John S. Dickerson's schooner Madeline was selected as the sole defender and won in succession the two races required. Since both schooners were of the same centerboard type these races were not as significant as the previous ones.

The opening of the Union Pacific Railroad in 1869 greatly increased the accessibility of the West and the ease of shipment from the West. This created a much wider interest in sport on the prairies and in the Rockies, but it also made possible the sending of buffalo hides and other skins from the far prairies to the eastern markets. As a result, we begin to get, side by side with descriptions of western sport, accounts of the slaughter of the buffaloes for their hides.

In 1870 the illustrated papers begin to include pictures of life on the plains, of deer racing a locomotive, of a train being stopped by herds

[165]

of buffaloes, and of another train pausing to permit passengers to shoot at antelopes. Then in 1872 and 1874 *Harper's Weekly* pictured the slaughter of the buffaloes and the shipping of their hides.

To sportsmen two of the saddest chapters in the history of American game have been the extermination of the passenger pigeons, which once flew in millions, and of the buffaloes which roamed in thousands. But it should be remembered that their very numbers made them unadaptable to the development of the country. To agriculture the vast flocks of pigeons were a scourge and they had to be driven away or killed. On the prairies there could be no cattle ranges where the buffaloes grazed, and perhaps their elimination was a necessary prelude to the ranches.

Whether pigeons and buffaloes had to exist in huge numbers or not at all is a question for evolutionists. The great flock or herd is a protection against some enemies, but it precludes hiding from others. Perhaps pigeons and buffaloes had both depended too much on numbers and had never learned to conceal themselves. Certainly concealment and not numbers would have been the better protection against the new conditions introduced by the civilization of the white man.

The wholesale killing of the buffaloes was looked upon by the Indians as a destruction of their food supply and led to bloody uprisings, but it has also been stated that it enabled the government for the first time to hold the Indians to their reservations.

For decades, however, there were still enough buffaloes and other game in the West for sportsmen, while the railroads, which soon entered the Southwest and Northwest, as well as the West, made sporting trips more practicable. Highly considered in the seventies were turkey hunting in Texas, antelope and prairie chicken shooting on the prairies, bear trailing in the Rockies, and elk hunting on the Upper Missouri. A sport peculiar to Texas and suited only to reckless riders, was the chase of a deer across the fallen timbers that characterized certain sections of the state.

In the South there were deer driving and bear hunting. In the North

Hunting antelopes in the West, 1874

Shooting antelopes from a train in Colorado, 1875

there was good deer hunting in Michigan and Wisconsin, and moose were plentiful in Nova Scotia. In the East deer were still shot on Long Island and more frequently in the Adirondacks. Ducks were abundant, though the canvasbacks were confined to near the Chesapeake. Geese and swans were common in certain sections and seasons. Grouse, quail, and other game birds were still to be found in suitable districts not too far from sizeable cities.

Rifle shooting was still feeling the impetus given it by the war, and the National Rifle Association was organized in 1871. Two years later the association, encouraged by the government, purchased Creedmoor, on Long Island, as a practice range. Under the auspices of the Centennial and the government, the association held there in 1876 a great national rifle match, — the first in this country.

After a series of matches for individual supremacy, there was a national team match between the Americans, Irish, Scots, Australians, and Canadians. The distances were 800, 900, and 1000 yards and each team shot twice from each distance. In the first time around the Australians were first at 800 yards, the Scots first at 900 yards, and the Scots and Irish tied at 1000 yards. As the second round progressed it was seen that the match for the total number of points would be very close. At 800 yards the Scots and Americans were tied for first, at 900 yards the Americans led, and at 1000 yards the Irish were first, Mr. Milner of their team hitting the bull's-eye every shot. Out of a possible 3,600 points, the American team made 3,126 and won the match, the Irish being only 22 points behind.

The revival of foxhunting near New York City probably grew out of the fact that about 1874 Colonel Frederick S. Skinner and Mr. Joseph Donahue had a pack of hounds near Hackensack, and used to turn them loose after foxes on the New Jersey Meadows, while they followed the chase with a horse and buggy. The next year a few riders got the habit of coming across from New York to join the chase, and in 1876 there was a large field.

In 1877 A. Belmont Purdy, William E. Peet, F. Gray Griswold, and Robert Center met and subscribed $1000 with which Mr. Griswold, who was going abroad, was to purchase a pack of hounds; in the meantime they leased a farm at Meadow Brook. The first meeting of their Queens County Hounds was dated October 4, 1877. Mr. Griswold was Master of Hounds, of which there were seventeen couples, and there were from forty to fifty riders.

The meets were very successful the first year, the farmers profiting from the interest, but the second year there were various objections, and the pack was moved to Westchester County, Mr. Griswold eventually becoming sole owner.

In the meantime there began to be calls for a renewal of foxhunting at Meadow Brook. Mr. Purdy supported a pack in 1880 at his own expense, then in 1881 the Meadow Brook Hunt was incorporated.

At about that date also, Mr. Griswold, finding the terrain too rough in Westchester, returned to Long Island with the Queens County Hounds, while packs were organized at various other locations near New York.

At Newport, for the last hunt of the season of 1879, according to *Harper's Weekly*, "all Newport mustered at the meet, the road to South-wick's Grove being literally choke-full of vehicles of every sort, shape, size, and description." Ladies were in the most "eel-like" habits. They were carefully piloted but one or two steered for themselves. The brush went to Mr. Fairman Rogers, "whose get up reminded one of a picture by Herring," for being first at the kill, while Miss Havemeyer and Miss Oouthout received recognition because they "rode from the burst to the death."

The most celebrated running horses of the seventies were, with few exceptions, sired by either Lexington or Imported Leamington. Among Lexington's get were Harry Bassett, Monarchist, and Foster; among Leamington's were Longfellow, Enquirer, Aristides, Parole, and Iroquois.

Enquirer won every race as a three-year-old, but soon afterward

*Last meet of the season of the Queens County Hunt
at Southwick's Grove, near Newport, 1870*

The opening day at Jerome Park, 1876

struck himself and was retired. Longfellow was probably the most celebrated horse of the decade. He was a big brown, 17 hands high, and raw-
boned. He was distanced by Enquirer in his first race in the spring of
1870, but in the fall won five straight races. The next year he defeated
Kingfisher for the Saratoga Cup. In 1872, at Long Branch, he defeated
Harry Bassett in a great race before 30,000 people, but later, in the race
for the Saratoga Cup, he lost half of one of his front plates and in turn
was beaten by Harry Bassett. He pulled up lame and was retired. Harry
Bassett was also winner of the Travers and Belmont Stakes in 1871. He
and Monarchist, both sons of Lexington, won and lost against each other,
Monarchist, when he won, having to run full speed from the start.

Another son of Lexington was Foster. He was foaled in 1867 and
won several matches in the East, later being shipped out to the Pacific
coast. In 1876 there was a $30,000 purse offered for four-mile heats in
California. Captain Moore, who had an interest in Foster, had brought
Wildidle from the East to enter it, but Wildidle had broken down. As a
last resort Moore sent up into Oregon for Foster, who was then nine years
old. They trained him with gallops of two miles repeated until at last his
muscles and his wind strengthened. The race was conceded to Lucky
Baldwin's Rutherford, but old Foster won in two straight heats.

The winner of the first Kentucky Derby in 1875, and of the Withers
Stake, was Aristides, son of Leamington. The next year he defeated Ten
Broeck, the best horse of the West at any distance of from one to four
miles.

Ten Broeck was bred by John Harper of Kentucky. He was sired by
Imported Phaeton and foaled by Fanny Holton in 1872. He raced only
once as a two-year-old, and as a three-year-old won and lost at the shorter
distances, but won regularly in the two-mile and three-mile heat races
that called for endurance. In 1876 he won eight out of nine races. On
September 23rd, in the Post Stakes, he ran three miles in 5:26½, which
was a record. This encouraged his owner to send him against Fellow-
craft's four-mile record of 7:19½ made at Saratoga in 1874. Ten Broeck

ran the first mile in 1:52½, which was the slowest one of the four, but made the first two miles in 3:38, the three in 5:24½, and the four in 7:15¾, which was the first reduction of the record by seconds since Lexington's day.

Another of the descendants of Leamington was Parole, a gelding and a great campaigner. When four years old he defeated Ten Broeck and Tom Ochiltree of Baltimore. Then he was taken to England with Duke of Magenta, who as a three-year-old had won eleven of twelve races but unfortunately on this trip came down with influenza. Parole retrieved the fortunes of the stable by winning five important races. In 1880 he won four races at Jerome Park, right after landing from the boat. Between 1875 and 1884 he was in 137 races, winning 59 of them and $82,909 in money.

Spendthrift was one of the few famous horses from a different strain. He was sired by Imported Australian and foaled in 1876. In 1878 he won all his races, which were in the West. At three years he was sold to Mr. Keene and brought east. He won the Belmont Stakes, and though left at the post in the Lorillard Stakes, and fifty yards behind, won anyway. He had trouble with his feet and was retired. From him are descended Fair Play and Man O'War.

In 1870 a little football of the association type was being played at a dozen of the eastern colleges, and a few intercollegiate games took place, in which Princeton defeated Rutgers, and the latter revenged itself on Columbia. There were no intercollegiate games the next year, but a few in 1872.

In 1873 a convention was held October 18th, to formulate rules in which Princeton, Columbia, Yale, and Rutgers concurred, but Harvard did not.

The practical introduction of Rugby football came in 1874, when McGill University came down from Montreal and played Harvard two games. The first was under Harvard rules, but the second, on May 15th, was under the All-Canada Rugby rules. Harvard tied the score and was

Trotting in Harlem Lane, 1870

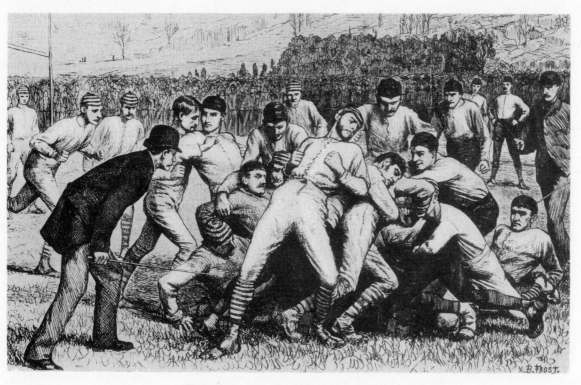

Yale-Princeton football match in 1879

At the Club House, Jerome Park, 1875

very much impressed by the Rugby game. In October the Harvard team visited Montreal and defeated the McGill University team.

In 1875 Harvard and Tufts played a Rugby game which Tufts won, special football suits appearing, it is said, upon the field for the first time.

In 1876, November 23rd, an Intercollegiate Football Association was formed by Harvard, Princeton, and Columbia, which adopted the British Rugby Union rules. There were fifteen players on a side. A curious phase of the scoring was that it took four touchdowns to equal a goal. Thus Yale defeated Harvard by a field goal, though Harvard scored two touchdowns. In the Princeton game Walter Camp of Yale passed the ball to Thompson, who scored. Thereupon the referee tossed a coin to decide on its legality.

In 1879 Yale joined Harvard and Princeton in an intercollegiate series, playing Rugby rules and fifteen men to a side.

A highly important game invented in the seventies was lawn tennis. Devised by Major Walter Wingfield in England in the fall of 1873, as a modification of court tennis for garden parties, the game was soon taken to the British garrison at Bermuda, from where a set was brought to New York by Miss Mary Ewing Outerbridge, probably in the spring of 1874. One of her brothers was a director of the Staten Island Cricket and Base Ball Club and through him she received permission to lay out a court in a corner of the club's grounds.

The next year, 1875, a set was imported by William Appleton, and the game tried out on his grounds at Nahant, Massachusetts, by Dr. James Dwight, who was later president of the United States Lawn Tennis Association for many years, and F. R. Sears, brother of the first national champion.

The game as it came to America differed greatly in many technical details from the game of to-day. In the beginning, the server stood in a small square in the middle of one court and served over the net and beyond the service line into the back of the other court, nor was he put back to the baseline until the spring of 1875. Also the counting was at first on the racquets system, only the server scoring and 15 being game, each point counting one.

The first women players merely patted the ball to and fro, and many of the men did little more. But some of the cricket and baseball players batted away at it, only to discover that they had no control over the ball. The great significance of the innovation, however, was that here was a game that could be played by women, which was nevertheless more active than croquet, or baseball, or cricket, and therefore interesting to men.

The game was soon taken to Philadelphia, and in the first number of the *American Cricketer* was described as being popular at the cricket clubs there.

The lawns of the cricket clubs were suited to tennis and it was easily adopted, but soon there began to be grumblings from the old cricketers that tennis was luring the young fellows away from cricket practice. Letters complaining about this appeared in the *American Cricketer;* other correspondents answered that tennis was bringing new blood into the clubs.

Both sides were right. In the years to come, tennis and cricket were unconsciously to fight it out for popularity at the Germantown Cricket Club, the Merion Cricket Club, the Longwood Cricket Club, and the Staten Island Cricket and Base Ball Club. Cricket died; perhaps tennis helped to kill it, but it saved the clubs. These great clubs still exist, but they are now tennis clubs; the "Cricket" in their names is but little more than a memory, — an anachronism from a past age.

The application of four rollers to "parlor skates," by J. L. Plimpton in 1863, made them more easily managed, and in 1865 there were a few small rinks in the East. At that time the new skates were taken up by William H. Fuller, an adventurous young man who had been captain of a ship to China, sewing-machine expert in England, and ice skater in New York. He learned to do fancy figures on them and was taken by George Coppin to Australia where he started a vogue for roller skating. From there Fuller gave skating exhibitions around the world, in India,

Opening day of the Ladies' Athletic Club, Staten Island, 1877

The Polo Club House and grounds at Jerome Park, 1876

Colonel Delancey Kane's New Rochelle and Pelham coach starting
from the Hotel Brunswick, Madison Square, New York, 1876

Turkey, Greece, Russia from Odessa to St. Petersburg, Germany and Holland. He introduced his program with a conception of the helpless Lord Dundreary learning to skate, and gave special parties for children. It was five years before he returned to the United States, to find that the rage he had started in Australia, had been carried to England and was reappearing in America.

In the seventies the craze spread like wildfire over the country, carried, it is true, by special exhibitors, who moreover helped to fit up halls as rinks, in which the sport could continue after their departure. It lent itself not only to graceful attitudes which could be portrayed in the periodicals, but to every variety of fall that could be caricatured by comic artists.

During the early seventies Goldsmith Maid was still queen of the trotting tracks. In 1871 she defeated Lucy at Milwaukee, lowering Dexter's record to 2:17, and reduced this by a fraction the next year. In 1874 she put the trotting record below 2:15 for the first time, defeating Judge Fullerton and American Girl in 2:14¾, and finally lowered her mark to 2:14. At nineteen she again equalled this record. She died in 1885 at the age of twenty-eight, and on her tombstone near Trenton, New Jersey, it is engraved that she earned $364,200, which in 1931 is still the world's record for any horse.

The Grand Circuit for trotting races was established in 1873, including Cleveland, Buffalo, Utica, and Springfield. Two years later Rochester and Poughkeepsie joined and it became the Central Circuit.

Goldsmith Maid's record was lowered to 2:13¼ by Rarus in 1878, and to 2:12¾ by St. Julian the next year, then with the eighties followed the era of Maud S.

Coaching, which had passed out of existence in the East, except in reaching a few mountain resorts, was revived as a sport by Colonel Delancey Kane. He was the pioneer amateur coachman of New York City and in May, 1876, inaugurated a coaching line from New York to New Rochelle, Pelham, and return.

Although he was strictly a gentleman whip, bookings were made at the Hotel Brunswick and a fare of two dollars was charged for the trip. Promptly at 10:30 every morning except Sunday, with a punctuality that marked the enterprise, he gathered up the reins of his four-horse team and set out with his fashionable party.

Soon afterwards a coaching club was organized in which twenty-one coaches were represented. An official dress was selected, which consisted of a dark green cutaway with brass buttons and a yellow striped waist-coat. The evening costume was of the same colors, but with a full dress coat. A parade was held each year on the last Saturday in May, meeting in Madison Square and driving up Fifth Avenue and around Central Park.

Other coaching lines were inaugurated to points of interest, including one to Philadelphia; the four-in-hand became an important adjunct to mountain resorts, and coaching became a favorite method of taking the air and sight-seeing for more than a decade.

The first of the annual bench shows of dogs in New York was given by the Westminster Kennel Club in 1877. It was held at Gilmore's Garden between Madison and Fourth Avenues and 26th and 27th Streets.

The sporting dogs included English, Irish, and Gordon setters, and black and tan, or black and white setters. There were likewise pointers, Chesapeake dogs, Irish water spaniels, Cocker spaniels, field spaniels, and other retrievers. Other classes were for foxhounds and harriers in couples, and for beagles, staghounds, deerhounds, and greyhounds.

Outside the sporting classes were mastiffs, St. Bernards and terriers, and those characteristic products of the period, pug dogs and poodles.

While polo had been played in India since mediaeval times, it was not until the sixties that it was brought by British officers, who learned it in India, to England. In 1876 it was introduced into the United States by James Gordon Bennett who promoted the Westchester Polo Club, and advanced capital for grounds and a clubhouse adjacent to Jerome Park. The game was at once recognized by the periodicals as active and exciting. The *Daily Graphic* said of it, in June, 1876:

The first annual bench show of dogs at the Hippodrome, 1877

A match game of the Westchester Polo Club at their grounds at Jerome Park, 1876

[184]

"It is easy to see how health giving that game [polo] is to the physical man, calling, as it does, every nerve and sinew of the body into vigorous play. It is picturesque, too, and a fine thing to look at. Mr. James Gordon Bennett is the prime mover in the introduction of polo into this country, and of course its great pillar and patron, having secured the grounds where it is played and spent a great deal of money in its furtherance. . . . The game is the most aristocratic in the world but cannot be played by those who, properly speaking, are the *jeunesse dorée* of the day."

That first summer Mr. Bennett offered a cup to the championship team which should be chosen by lot from the eighteen playing members. There were to be five on a team, and the object was to score the most goals in 1¾ hours. The ponies were then limited to fourteen hands, and in fact were the best Mexican mustangs.

When depicting one of these games *Harper's Weekly* wrote:

"The exhilarating and healthful game of polo has already become quite popular among New Yorkers, and a large number of invited spectators gathered at the grounds of the Westchester Polo Club at Jerome Park on the afternoon of June 6th, to witness the first of a series of match games to be played for the Challenge Cup, presented to the club by its president, J. G. Bennett, Esq. The club grounds were in fine order and the playing was very spirited."

A little later the game was being played at Manhattan Avenue and 110th Street at the Polo Grounds, that were named after it, and soon afterwards at Newport.

The most important development in baseball in the seventies was its establishment as a professional sport.

The new amateur association, which had attempted to keep the professionals out of amateur baseball, lasted only from 1872 to 1874, and since then there has been no national baseball organization endeavoring to enforce amateurism. The only serious efforts of this kind have been made by the colleges and schools.

In 1870 business men of Rockford, Illinois, realizing the publicity its great team, the Forest Citys, was gaining for the town, raised $7,000 to pay its expenses on a trip east, during which it won 51 of the 65 games played. This was still an amateur team, as amateurism was then defined.

That same year the highly successful professional team, the Cincinnati Red Stockings, broke up, and Harry Wright of that team gathered together a frankly professional team for Boston. Among them were A. G. Spalding, pitcher, and Ross Barnes, catcher, for the Forest Citys. In their first few games it was demonstrated that there was no prejudice in the East against professional ball playing. The National Association of Professional Base Ball Players was organized in 1871, but its schedules were loosely kept, and in 1876 it was superseded by the National League, which is still in existence. The members of the league the first year were the Athletics of Philadelphia, Hartford, Boston, Chicago, Cincinnati, Louisville, St. Louis, and the Mutuals of New York. The first president was Morgan G. Bulkley, afterward Connecticut governor and senator.

The introduction of professional baseball halted further development of the large social and amateur baseball clubs, which welcomed anyone interested in the game. It ended the growth of baseball as a social game, and substituted its development as a contest to be supported by the spectators. It encouraged semi-professionalism in the town teams, where perhaps the pitcher and catcher might be paid or found jobs for playing, and the others not. It tended to take the question of amateurism out of the game entirely, so that amateurs and semi-professionals played side by side or against each other without hesitation or consideration.

On the other hand, the National League did its best to keep the game played honestly. The second president, William A. Hulbert, expelled four players for throwing games. The league insisted that the games be won on their merits; it kept out the gamblers, forbade the players betting, and put a stop to their jumping from club to club, which was more than even the amateur association had been able to do.

Events of the Spring meeting of the New York Athletic Club at Mott Haven, 1876

ATHLETIC GAMES

1870-1890

ONE of the significant movements in the seventies and eighties was the rise of athletics, which had been practically unknown here as a sport for adults. The first and leading association was the New York Athletic Club, promoted by John C. Babcock, H. E. Buermeyer, and William B. Curtis. It gave an athletic meeting each year after its founding in 1868, and from 1876 to 1878 staged the annual championship. This drew a large number of spectators and was successful financially, but involved too much work for the officers. So in 1879 Mr. Goodwin and Mr. White organized the National Association of Amateur Athletics, of which the first president was Mr. George W. Carr of the Manhattan Club. Each club joining the association was to give at least one meeting a year. In 1880 fourteen sizeable clubs were members.

Most of the championship meetings were held at the grounds of the New York Athletic Club at Mott Haven, just north of the Harlem River, but in 1882 the meet was held at the old Polo Grounds at 110th Street, in order to give the college students a better opportunity to enter. The New York Athletic Club in 1887 acquired its grounds at Travers Island, named from William R. Travers, who was president of the club for the previous five years.

The year 1887 was enlivened by the presence of several celebrated English athletes. For comparative purposes it is interesting to note how some of the American records stood the next year. The time for the hundred yards was 10 seconds flat, for the 220 yards 22 seconds, and for the quarter mile 47¾ seconds. All of these, and especially the last, were not so far from the records to-day, but the best time then for the half mile was 1:55 2/5, and for the mile 4:21 2/5, which is considerably slower than now. However, they did ten miles, which had been a favorite distance in the old professional running matches, in 52:58 3/5.

The record for the running high jump then was 6:4, and for the pole vault for height 11:5. The latter, requiring technical skill in the management of the pole, was more than 2½ feet lower than at present.

Several of the other tests, such as putting the "heavy stone," and throwing the weight, are not comparable in records with to-day because under different conditions. The record for the running broad jump without weights was actually higher then than now, but the take-off was different.

In 1885 the athletic association passed a new and detailed rule concerning amateurism, and continued to do all it could to enforce it.

The rowing clubs were still numerous in the seventies and eighties. At a meeting of twenty-eight clubs in 1872 the first official definition of an amateur was formulated, and the next year the National Association of Amateur Oarsmen of the United States was organized. National championship regattas were held every year, beginning in 1873, at different rowing centers in the country, including Philadelphia, Troy, Detroit, Newark, Saratoga, Washington and Boston.

Included in the National Association were several local associations, such as the Northwestern at Detroit, the Mississippi Valley at Chicago, the Harlem River, the Passaic River, and the Schuylkill Navy.

In 1870 Yale first used a sliding seat, which was invented by Walter Brown, the professional sculler. That year Harvard won from Yale on a foul, and the next year they did not race, as the Rowing Association of American Colleges was organized in 1871. This held five regattas by 1875, but, as that year there were sixteen crews entered, forcing the rowing of heats. Harvard and Yale withdrew the next year and instituted their races with eight-oared boats over a four-mile straight-away course.

The association was reorganized as the Intercollegiate Rowing Asso-

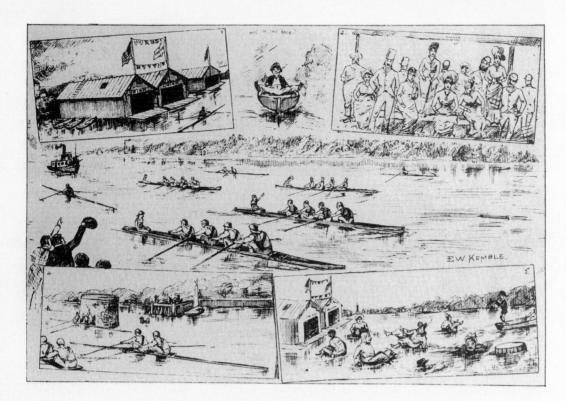

Second annual meeting of the Union Boat Club of Harlem, 1880

The Yale-Harvard boat race at New London, 1881

[191]

ciation with seven eastern colleges as members, and its races became a feature of the sport.

In 1878 Columbia sent its four-oared crew to England to try for the Visitors' Challenge Cup. The crew consisted of E. Sage, C. Edson, H. G. Ridabock, and J. T. Goodwin, stroke oar, with Charles Eldridge, substitute. The first heat, rowed on July 4th, was the harder, but Columbia defeated the Jesus College crew of Cambridge University after an exciting race. In the final heat the bow oarsman of the Hertford College crew collapsed and Columbia won by half a mile. When the crew returned to New York it was hauled up Broadway by the students and there was a great celebration.

The Childs' Cup races, which were open to university and college four-oared boats without coxswains, were inaugurated in 1879, but in 1889 the boats were changed from four oars to eight.

In 1881 Yale tried a short, fast stroke and won over Harvard in a hard race, by six seconds. Rowing a similar stroke the next year she lost to Harvard by three seconds in one of the closest races ever rowed between college crews in America, probably through being forced somewhat out of her course.

Thereafter both the Yale and Harvard stroke began to emphasize a long slide and leg work rather than arm work. Yale led for the decade of the eighties, winning seven times and losing thrice.

The greatest professional oarsman of the decade following the Centennial was Edward Hanlon. He was born in Toronto in 1855 and, beginning to row at eighteen, at twenty-one went to the Centennial at Philadelphia and won the single-scull championship of the United States in a series of heats against the best oarsmen of that day. The final heat, covering three miles with a turn, was rowed in 21:09, which created a new record.

The greatest sculling race of that era was Hanlon's match with Charles E. Courtney in 1878. Courtney was born at Union Springs, New York, in 1849, and at nineteen appeared for a race at Aurora, New

York, in a boat he had built himself. The spectators laughed at it, but he won anyway. He won 88 races as an amateur, and then in 1877 turned professional.

Hanlon and Courtney were matched for $11,000 in a purse and side bets, to row five miles over the Lachine Course near Montreal. Hanlon was five feet eight, and weighed 152 pounds; Courtney was over four inches taller, and fourteen pounds heavier.

At the start Hanlon was rowing 31 strokes to the minute, and Courtney 33. They were even at the mile in seven minutes. Hanlon was ahead at two miles and rounded the half-way mark first by five seconds. At the end of the third mile they were even again. The fourth mile was very fast but they still kept side by side. For the last mile Hanlon was rowing 33 strokes to the minute, while Courtney raised his beat to 36. It was a desperate finish, but Hanlon lasted better and "swept over the line, winner of the greatest single-scull race ever seen in this country, amid the deafening cheers of the assembled multitudes and the screech of the steam whistles."

Another match was arranged, but in the night before the race Courtney's boat was sawed in two by a saw inserted between the cracks of the boathouse.

Hanlon was never beaten until he went to Australia in 1884 and met Beech. He was for a time the coach at Columbia, while Courtney was the coach of the Cornell crew for many years.

The high-wheeled bicycle, which was invented in England in 1871, was exhibited at the Centennial Exposition in 1876. Gradually a few began to be sold in this country, while A. A. Pope of Boston, after taking two trips to England to study them, started their manufacture in the United States, as the later famous Columbia bicycle.

The first bicycle club in the metropolis was the New York Bicycle Club, which was organized in the fall of 1879, and was followed the same season by the Columbia Club. Several others, including the Mercury, Lenox, and Elite, were organized the next year.

*Trial of speed between Miss Elsa von Blumen, on a bicycle, and the trotting mare
"Hattie R," at Rochester, 1881*

*Wheelmen in Boston being reviewed by the Commander
on Commonwealth Avenue, 1881*

The New York Bicycle Club had a uniform which consisted of a cap ornamented with a winged wheel, a cadet-grey short coat with scarlet trimmings, and knee breeches, while the other clubs favored different colors.

The growth of cycling and tennis, both new sports, is indicated by the fact that the *American Cricketer*, founded in 1877 especially for cricket, began to notice tennis at once and on March 13th, 1880, stated that it would "embrace boating, tennis, bicycling, and other outdoor sports," and changed its heading to include them.

In the spring of 1880, the captain of the New York Bicycle Club suggested the first grand meeting of American wheelmen, and on Decoration Day thirty-one clubs met at Newport, Rhode Island. There they organized the League of American Wheelmen, which, along with the rapid spread of bicycling over the country, quickly developed into a far flung movement. It encouraged club runs, century runs, exhibitions of riding, and bicycle races, tried to keep the sport on a high plane, and assisted immeasurably in creating a short but notable era in transportation. The rubber tire was first developed for the bicycle. It was a solid strip to begin with, but later was superseded by a pneumatic tube which was afterwards taken over by the automobile.

The sight of the rider precariously perched on a towering wheel, caught the fancy of the artists and cartoonists, and there are numerous woodcuts of bicyclers in the periodicals. Their formal processions at their annual meetings in Boston or on Riverside Drive, New York; a woman bicycle rider racing a horse; bicycle races at fair grounds; how the bicycle scared the horses; the difficulties of learning to ride, and the header over the front wheel, are all depicted among other cycling subjects in the illustrated press.

Professional pedestrianism had quite a flair in the seventies and eighties. Edward Payson Weston was the most widely known of the walkers but was beaten several times in the go-as-you-please races.

In 1878 Sir John Astley, a member of parliament and a well known sportsman, offered £500 and the Astley Belt to the winner of a six-day go-as-you-please race. The first race under these conditions was held in that year and won by Daniel O'Leary, who had beaten Weston in 1877.

Challenges and races followed one after another. In October, 1878, O'Leary defeated John Hughes by 403 miles to 310.

The fifth contest for the Astley Belt representing the long distance championship of the world was held at Madison Square beginning Monday morning, September 22nd, 1879. There was a large crowd present and many bets were made on the outcome. There were thirteen contestants and the progress of each one was shown on a recording dial in view of the grandstand. Weston held the record of 530 miles in six days, and for this and other reasons was the favorite, but soon got into difficulties and finished fifth. The race was won by Charles Powell of England, who approximated Weston's record for the six days.

The interest in marksmanship was maintained throughout the seventies and eighties. Captain A. H. Bogardus, who was born in New York State but had removed to Elkhart, Illinois, in 1856, began to make a local reputation there for his shooting, and in 1870 challenged Ira Paine of New York, who was then considered the leader at trap shooting, to a match. The contest took place on Long Island in January, 1871, and Paine won; but later in the year Bogardus defeated him by 87 to 86 birds, and held the badge given by L. L. Lorillard for the champion trap shooter for almost a quarter of a century.

In 1876 Paine improved on the spring trap to throw glass balls, and Bogardus demonstrated it in Gilmore's Garden by breaking 1,000 balls in 1 hour and 42 minutes.

The halo of the Wild West began to be thrown around marksmanship and wonderful tales made their way east as to the dead shots of the prairies and the mining camps. In 1878 Dr. W. F. Carver of California came east and gave exhibitions of shooting balls in the air from the back of a running horse. He was the forerunner of the Wild West Show, which still continues to dazzle the imagination of youth.

Quoit contest between Douglas and Pearson at Newark, N. J., 1874

The fifth contest for the long-distance pedestrian championship of the world at the Madison Square Garden, 1879

In 1886 the National Gun Club gave the first national tournament for trap shooters, who were selected by preliminary contests in the different states.

While baseball was turning professional in the seventies and eighties, cricket remained amateur. The cricket games were not so short, close, and exciting as baseball, and therefore not so capable of drawing crowds of paying spectators day after day. So the cricketers had less temptation than the ball players to develop professional teams.

But the game was just as interesting to the players as baseball and much more social, and the cricket clubs were reasonably prosperous for the two decades between 1870 and 1890.

Just as before the war, a great element of this interest and prosperity was international play. In 1872, W. G. Grace, the famous cricketer, brought over his eleven, and played several games here and in Canada. Two years later the Halifax Cup was won by a picked team from Philadelphia playing against Canadians. On the Philadelphia eleven were three of the celebrated Newhall brothers, among the best known of all American players. This cup was afterward the prize played for by the association of cricket clubs of Philadelphia.

Intercollegiate cricket was started in 1874 between Haverford and Pennsylvania.

In 1877 Daniel Newhall helped to found the *American Cricketer*, which was the authority and news sheet on the game, and afterward, beginning in March, 1880, on amateur sports in general.

The next year an eleven from Australia met eighteen men picked from New York clubs, which was the method employed in cricket of evening the teams. The match was played at the St. George's Cricket Club grounds at Hoboken. J. E. Sprague, an old baseball pitcher, who bowled for the New Yorkers, surprised the Australians, but they won, 162 to 161, with five wickets to spare.

The Philadelphia cricket clubs in 1879 sent a picked team to Great Britain, where it did well in Ireland, Scotland, and against the average county clubs in England. That same year international games with Canada were resumed, and aroused general interest.

In the eighties there were reported to be twenty cricket clubs in the neighborhood of New York. The largest were the St. George's at Hoboken, the Staten Island Base Ball and Cricket Club, the Manhattan, and the Seabright. At Philadelphia, which was the strongest center of cricket in America, were the Philadelphia Cricket Club, the Germantown, the Merion, the Belmont, and the Young America, all important clubs not only for cricket but socially. In Boston, there was especially the Longwood Cricket Club.

But in spite of the hold cricket had in certain districts, it did not "take" throughout the country, nor spread as did baseball or tennis. The cricket clubs could allow for both amateur baseball and tennis, but when golf came along, their grounds were not large enough to include it, and they had to turn to tennis to meet its competition for members.

Coaches at Jerome Park on a race day, 1886

IN THE EIGHTIES

IN the decade between 1880 and 1890 there were four challenges for
the cup won by the America. The first was from the Bay of Quinte
Yacht Club of Belleville, Ontario, with the Atalanta, which was a
centerboard sloop of the type then favored in the United States. The
New York Yacht Club was rather shocked when the Atalanta was towed
to New York through the canals and down the Hudson. She was defeated
decisively by the Mischief, an iron sloop designed by A. Cary Smith and
owned by J. R. Busk. Afterward it was ruled that the challenging yacht
must proceed under sail on her own bottom to the locality of the contest.

The next challenge was from Sir Richard Sutton, of the Royal Yacht
Squadron, with the cutter Genesta. She was one of the most extreme of
the plank-on-edge type. To meet her the Puritan, designed by Edward
Burgess of Boston, won the test against the Priscilla, designed by A. Cary
Smith. In the Puritan, Burgess sought to combine the best features of
centerboard sloop and cutter. She had a centerboard but also a lead keel
and considerable depth, while her rig was more like that of a cutter than
of a sloop. She won the test against the Priscilla, and went on to defeat
the Genesta in two races. The first race was won by over 16 minutes, but
the second one by only a minute and 38 seconds, which was the narrowest
margin of any of the races up to that time.

The scene at the beginning of the last race was described by *Leslie's
Weekly* as follows:

"The second and final race, on Wednesday the 16th inst., was much
more exciting than the first. . . . To the satisfaction of everyone there was

a fresh wind and plunging sea from the start. In fact the weather was all that the Genesta's friends had asked for. A fine squadron of excursion boats and pleasure boats went down the Bay to witness what proved to be one of the most superb races ever sailed in New York waters."

The final race was twenty miles to leeward and return. The Genesta rounded the outer mark first by a couple of minutes. On the return the wind shifted somewhat and the twenty miles in was made in two tacks, a long leg and a short one. The race was evidently very close. According to *Leslie's Weekly*, "Both yachts came down to the finish in magnificent style, — the cutter made a gallant fight for it, but the Puritan swept over the goal a winner."

In 1886 Lieutenant William Henn of the Royal Navy challenged with the Galatea of the Royal Northern Yacht Club, but she was defeated by General Paine's Mayflower. Though the American and British type of yachts were approaching each other, *Harper's Weekly* hailed the victory as a proof of the superiority of the centerboard design:

"The result of the two races between Lieutenant Henn's British cutter Galatea and General Paine's sloop Mayflower for the America's Cup on the 7th and 9th of September, once more conclusively proves that the light displacement centerboard yacht is faster than the deep and narrow cutter of great displacement."

The next year, 1887, the Royal Clyde Yacht Club challenged with the Thistle which had been designed by George L. Watson to take advantage of the new rules of measurement. She was met by the Volunteer, another yacht designed by Edward Burgess and owned by General Paine, and defeated in two races. This seems to have convinced the English that recapturing the America's Cup was a difficult undertaking, and there were no more challenges for five years.

The high spot attained by polo in the eighties was the first international match against England, played at Newport in 1886. The Westchester Polo Club represented America, and the Hurlingham Polo Club, England.

The match, in which two countries played at one of the most ancient and kingly of games in America's most fashionable summer resort, was a great social event. The setting was thus described in *Harper's Weekly:*

"The first of the International polo playing took place at Newport on August 25. So striking a congregation of persons and things fashionable and fine is rarely to be met with. The grounds were lined with drags and carts, and all the catalogue of japanned and magnificent vehicles; there was no end of beautiful faces and the raiment was bewildering. The polo which was played before this notable company was between the Hurlingham Club of England and the Westchester Club of this city. The Englishmen wore satin shirts and jockey caps of light blue, white riding breeches and boots of russet leather. Their horses were not especially handsome but they were especially serviceable. The Americans wore light yellow jerseys and caps of the same color, their breeches and boots being the same as those of the Englishmen. The English players were Mr. John Watson, Captain Malcolm Little, Captain T. Hone, and Captain T. R. Lawley; the Americans, Mr. Thomas Hitchcock, Jun., Captain W. K. Thorn, Jun., Mr. Foxhall Keene, and Mr. R. R. Belmont."

Polo had been played in England about twice as many years as in America, and the British had developed team work, while the American play was more individualistic. As a consequence the Hurlingham team won very decisively, by ten goals to four the first day, and fourteen to two the second day.

Since the Civil War the character of the running races had been changing. The old standard four-mile race, two out of three heats, passed out of existence, and even the three-mile tests, which had been considered a concession to younger horses, were eliminated. The Saratoga Cup for three-year-olds and over, between 1865 and 1886 was one heat at $2\frac{1}{4}$ miles and was the longest of the big races. The Travers Stakes for three-year-olds at Saratoga was run in one heat at $1\frac{3}{4}$ miles from 1864 to 1889; the Belmont Stakes for three-year-olds was at $1\frac{5}{8}$ miles from 1867 to 1873, and at $1\frac{1}{2}$ from 1874 to 1889.

Heats were eliminated entirely, and the trend was more and more toward the use of younger horses, shorter races, and more contests a day. If this was brought about in part by a desire for more rapid turnover in the poolrooms, it led to its own punishment in a rising public sentiment that race meetings were run for the betting.

Another result was that the career of a running horse, instead of extending a decade as previously, became limited to a few years.

The first of the horses to stand out in the early eighties was Luke Blackburn, by Bonnie Scotland, of Lexington stock, foaled in 1877. He was hard to control but in 1880 he won nineteen out of twenty races for the Dwyer brothers. Even better was Hindoo, who was by Virgil, and also owned by the Dwyer brothers. He was foaled in 1878 by Florence, who was by Lexington. From a colt he was gentle and was managed without an effort, a direct contrast to Luke Blackburn in the same stables. In 1881 he won eighteen out of twenty races and was considered the best of his time.

The first American horse to win the English Derby was Iroquois, who was by Leamington and foaled in 1878. He was owned by Pierre Lorillard and taken to England when young. In 1881 he created one sensation after another by winning both the Derby and the St. Leger.

One of the biggest money earners of that decade was Miss Woodford, by Billet. In 1882 the Dwyers got her in exchange for Hindoo, who had retired. She raced for half a dozen years and won $118,270, which was a record for mares up to that time.

Another big winner of the eighties and a great horse was Hanover, by Hindoo. He was foaled in 1884 and raced until five years of age. He earned $118,872, and was the leading sire of the winning horses for each of the years from 1895 to 1898. At three years he twice defeated Kingston, who was sired by Spendthrift and himself earned $138,917 for the Dwyers. Some of Kingston's greatest races were with Firenzi, who was by Glenelg and succeeded Miss Woodford as queen of the turf, winning in all $112,586.

Sir Dixon, who, like Miss Woodford, was sired by Billet, was owned by Green B. Morris when as a two-year-old he beat Raceland, but the next year was sold to the Dwyer brothers for $20,000. At three he won both the Withers and the Belmont Stakes. At six he was retired to the stud, and was the leading sire of the winning horses of 1901. Raceland was himself the winner of seventy races and $116,391.

The winner of the first Futurity Stakes for two-year-olds was Proctor Knott, the best son of Luke Blackburn. He defeated Salvator in a driving finish by a short head, but the latter had the greater subsequent career.

Salvator, who was foaled in 1886, was by Imported Prince Charlie. At two years he won all the races but the one lost to Proctor Knott. At three he lost only one race, and that to Longstreet. At four he won all his races. He defeated Tenny in the Suburban, and a week later proved his right to do so by beating him in a match race for $5,000 a side. This race was so close that Isaac Murphy on Salvator and Garrison on Tenny both thought they had won. Other horses began to refuse to run against him, so at Monmouth Park, August 28th, 1890, he ran against time and lowered the mile record of 1:39¼ to 1:35½. In all in his short but brilliant racing career, he earned $113,710, and at five years was retired from the track.

The trotting queen of the eighties was Maud S. She was sired by Harold, of Hambletonian stock, and foaled in 1874 by Miss Russell, a granddaughter of Boston. Maud S. was bred by J. A. Alexander in Kentucky, and as a three-year-old was sold to Captain George N. Stone of Cincinnati. When four years old she trotted a trial at Lexington in 2:17½. This gave promise of her being a record breaker and she was sold to William H. Vanderbilt for $21,000. In 1880 she justified her price by trotting a mile in 2:10½, which was a new trotting record, and was a personal triumph for Mr. Vanderbilt because it bettered the times of Rarus and St. Julien, who were both owned by Robert Bonner. In 1883 Mr. Vanderbilt himself drove Maud S. and Aldine, his fancy road team, a mile in 2:15½, which broke the record.

Her supremacy was threatened in 1884 by Jay Eye See, who was by Dictator and descended from Hambletonian. On August 1st the shapely black gelding trotted a mile in 2:10 flat, reaching that coveted figure for the first time. But he occupied the throne for only one day, for on August 2nd, 1884, at Cleveland, Maud S. first broke 2:10 by trotting in 2:09¼.

This was too much for Robert Bonner, who liked to own the fastest trotters, and he managed to purchase her for $40,000 from Mr. Vanderbilt, who had been receiving numberless requests for exhibitions. She justified this purchase also by again breaking her record.

The effort was made at Cleveland, July 30th, 1885. It had rained in the early morning and the track was a trifle slow, but she liked the softness. It was nearly 5 p. m. when William W. Blair gave her a preliminary warming up in 2:26½. There were 12,000 spectators who cheered her when she appeared for the trial. She seemed to jump away from the wire and made the first half in 1:04½. "Around the turn she came, like the wind," wrote an eye witness in the *Spirit of the Times*. "Only once did the chestnut nose go up. All held their breath fearing that she would break, but Blair was seen to take her back, and away she went again, steady and true."

The time at the three-quarters was 1:35½. On the home stretch she faltered slightly, but Blair touched her with the whip and she flashed under the wire, going very fast. When the judges announced the time as 2:08¾, there was a tremendous cheer, and a rush for the trotting queen. A collar of roses was thrown about her neck, and she stepped as proudly as if she knew what she had done. Her record stood for five years, and was bettered but little until after the advent of the pneumatic, ball-bearing sulky.

As evident from facts already given, this was a great era for driving. When Robert Bonner was driving Dexter, Commodore Cornelius Vanderbilt was driving Myron Perry and Daisy Burns. Later Bonner drove Rarus, St. Julien, and Maud S., all record breakers, and was the most

Sleighing near McComb's Dam Bridge, 1880

[211]

celebrated owner and amateur driver of fast roadsters in the country. William H. Vanderbilt was no doubt second, and at times first among the amateur drivers.

There was a great deal of rivalry among the gentlemen drivers as to who should have the fastest team. William H. Vanderbilt in 1877 drove his well known pair, Lady Mac and Small Hopes, in 2:23, which was then the record. In 1881 John Shepard of Boston beat this by driving Blondine and Mill Boy to a road wagon in 2:22. A number of the New Yorkers tried to better this. T. E. Eastman drove his Glendale and Captain Jack in 2:24. E. Foster Dewey made 2:22¼ with William H. and Boston. Then William H. Vanderbilt bought William H. and putting him with Lysander, had Dan Mace drive them in 2:20. Frank Work countered by having Dick Swiveler and Edward driven by Mace in 2:19½.

The next year, in July, Shepherd F. Knapp bet Frank Work $1,000 that his team could not beat 2:20, so Work put John Murphy behind them and they did the mile in 2:16¾, which was a new record. The country was thereupon scoured for fast trotters that could step together. William H. Vanderbilt purchased Early Rose and Aldine and unofficially equalled the mark made by Work's team. The next year he bought Maud S. and putting her with Aldine reduced the record to 2:15½.

The celebrated drives were on upper Broadway, then called the Boulevard, on Riverside Drive, St. Nicholas Avenue, upper Eighth Avenue, for the time being called Central Avenue, and on Ocean Parkway from Prospect Park to Coney Island. For driving or trotting, and especially for trials at the records, there were Fleetwood Park near Melrose, the Brooklyn Driving Park, and Prospect Driving Park.

The fame of the great roadsters around New York spread throughout the North and was emulated everywhere. Indeed, little encouragement was necessary, because throughout all the rest of the North trotting races were more common than in New York City, and were a constant stimulation to driving.

[213]

The National Horse Show was inaugurated by the association of that name in 1883 in New York. Prominent among its promoters were Cornelius Fellowes, John G. Heckscher, H. H. Hollister, and W. F. Wharton. It was held at Madison Square Garden, which was prepared by removing the floor from the center and covering the surface with tanbark.

Besides the prizes for thoroughbreds, trotters, hunters, and saddle horses, there were special considerations for carriage horses and four-in-hands, which drew the fashionable turn-outs of that decade. And there were also prizes for fire engine horses, ponies, heavy draught horses, horses for general use, and for donkeys and mules. In all about $11,000 was offered in prizes and 350 horses were entered. The horse show was a social success from the beginning and became an established institution.

Various new phases of sport were given national prominence in the eighties.

A few of these came from Canada. Tobogganing was introduced at Saratoga and in Vermont early in the decade, and in 1885 the Essex County Toboggan Club built a slide near the Oranges, New Jersey. The slide was 1,004 feet long and only about four feet in width, and the toboggans were steered with the feet. The club dress for men was of colored wool, while the ladies wore blanket costumes in gay colors. In the evening when the slide was lighted with many lights it was said to present an animated and picturesque scene. Snowshoeing was experimented with as a stunt, but there was hardly enough snow around New York to give it a permanent hold. Lacrosse, the old Indian game, was brought down from Canada, and a game between Yale and New York is represented in *Harper's Weekly* in 1883. Hockey, which had already been played as roller polo, was introduced on ice at the end of the decade.

Parallel with tobogganing, coasting was developed at Albany, until the bobsleds were capable of holding a dozen or more, and were steered with a wheel. Several engravings show winter sports at Tuxedo, Lake Placid, and other places, and indicate that the development of the winter resort was taking place.

The National Horse Show at Madison Square Garden, 1883

[215]

The Essex County Country Club toboggan slide, 1886

Greyhound racing was introduced by 1884 at Philadelphia and elsewhere and was run under favorable auspices, having quite a vogue for a number of years.

Field trials of pointers and setters are pictured in American periodicals as early as 1878, but did not become national until later.

Many varieties of field sport were judged to be of wide enough interest to be illustrated in the national weeklies. In the first half of the eighties are shown ruffed grouse shooting, duck shooting on the Delaware and in the West, quail shooting, rabbit shooting on Long Island, moose hunting, a buffalo hunt, rail shooting, wild turkey calling, hunting on snowshoes, prairie chicken shooting, pigeon trapping on Coney Island, wild swan in North Carolina, protecting fields in California from wild geese, bears in the Adirondacks, hunting grizzlies in the Rockies, a coon hunt in Maryland, and hunting scenes in Wyoming.

In the latter part of the eighties the national weeklies depict, as of general interest, deer shooting from a platform, hunting woodcock, wild hog shooting in Arkansas, canvasback shooting on the Chesapeake, shooting pronghorns from a mustang, turkey hunting, shooting snipe and rail in Pennsylvania, a rabbit drive in California, deer hunting in Minnesota, and quail shooting on Long Island.

The fishing scenes that were apparently considered of national importance were not so many. They include blue fishing from the beach at Asbury Park and from an excursion boat; trout fishing on Long Island, in Maine and in Montana; angling for black bass, fishing in Pennsylvania, the perils of winter fishing, and shark fishing off New York.

Fresh water fishing around New York City in the eighties was pretty fully preëmpted by rather exclusive fishing clubs. Since there were over two million people within the present limits of New York City, and as in vacation and holiday time they were beginning to over-run most of the adjacent territory, it was a matter of controlling the trout fishing or having none at all.

On Long Island the little trout streams had been dammed to form ponds and the supply of trout was kept up by artificial stocking. The most expensive fishing coterie there was the Suffolk Club, which had a clubhouse near Patchogue. It fished exclusively for trout and only in artificial ponds. The initiation was $1500 and the membership was full. Then there was the Southside Club, which had a clubhouse near Oakdale, Long Island, and also fished only for trout in artificial ponds. The initiation was $1000, while the dues were by assessment. In 1884 there were still some memberships "open to gentlemen."

The Blooming Grove Park Club went to Pike County, Pennsylvania, where they fished for trout, bass, and pike, in natural waters, and without important stocking. For this reason their initiation was only $150 and their dues $75 a year. The Adirondack Club controlled a large tract in Essex County, New York, where they camped, hunted, and fished.

There were also several clubs that fished for sea bass in the Sound along the north side of Long Island, — among others, the Cuttyhunk, Pasque Island, No-man's-land, and Squibnocket.

If a man were a member of no club, he could go to Sayville, Long Island, and, by stopping at Foster's at $2.50 a day, fish with flies for trout in his pond. He could also go to Delaware Water Gap, 92 miles from New York, where he could fish for trout or other fish as pleased him, though accommodations were poor. There were also trout not far from Newburgh in the Navesink Creek.

The unattached fisherman could get bass fishing by going to the Van Sickland House at Coney Island at $3 a day and using crab bait in Coney Island Creek. There was spirited black bass fishing in Rye Lake in Westchester County, in Greenwood Lake, Orange County, and in Kinderhook Lake near Albany.

The best place for weakfish, with some striped bass, was in Newark Bay, near Newark Bridge, fishing from a boat and using shedder crabs for bait. Weakfish and bass were also caught at Robbins' Reef and Princess Bay.

There were, moreover, fishing boat excursions for blue fish off

Wild swan feeding on Currituck Sound, 1882

*The second Anglers' Tournament of the National Rod and Reel Association,
at Harlem Mere, Central Park, 1883*

[219]

The greyhound race at the fair of the State Agricultural Society at Philadelphia in 1884

Bay Shore, Long Island, and to other spots where fish of one sort or another were thought to be running.

A fly casting tournament for anglers was inaugurated in 1882. It was held at Harlem Mere, which was a pond at the north end of Central Park, under the auspices of the Rod and Reel Association.

The anglers came from all parts of the country, some of them as venerable as Rip Van Winkle. The rods were weighed and found to average about nine ounces, the lightest being eight and a half ounces. The casting was done from a platform over the pond. A line marked with numbered buoys was used to give direction and measure the distance cast, reaching to ninety feet. A small wooden disk was used as a target to test accuracy. There was a large attendance, including a goodly number of ladies, and a banquet at the Metropolitan Hotel, where the tournament was voted a success and made an annual event.

Pugilism began to arouse nation-wide attention again in the eighties. In 1880 Paddy Ryan defeated Joe Goss, ex-champion of England and claimant of the championship of the United States by a decision over Tom Allen on a foul, and Ryan was therefore considered champion. By this time a Boston strong boy, John L. Sullivan, was growing up and gaining local notoriety. He challenged Ryan, but was told to get a reputation, which he proceeded to do by winning several more local contests. The two were finally matched to fight near New Orleans in 1882.

Prize fighting was still done here under the old London prize ring rules and was against the law all over the country. In order to pull off the fight, the crowd was taken on February 7th, 1882, to Mississippi City, where the square was roped off. In the first round Sullivan leaped for Ryan and with the first blow knocked him down. The second round ended when Ryan threw Sullivan with a body hold, but Sullivan retaliated by throwing him with the same grip. From that time Sullivan led, and in the ninth round won by a knockout to the jaw.

Sullivan seems to have been the first pugilist to understand that the right blow to the jaw might produce a knock-out and a quick ending to the fight. At least he used this blow in many four-round boxing exhibitions with gloves, which he gave throughout the country.

Sullivan acquired a great reputation, and it was considered a feat to stand up before him. But Charlie Mitchell was a trouble maker. In an exhibition with gloves at Madison Square Garden in May, 1883, he caught Sullivan a little off balance and knocked him down in the first round. Sullivan had the best of the next two rounds, when the police interfered, as they did regularly when the exhibition looked as if it might develop into a fight or knockout. Dominick McCaffrey in 1885 gained repute by holding Sullivan for six rounds, and in 1887 Patsy Cardiff earned a draw, though Sullivan broke a bone in his arm in the third round.

On August 8, 1887, at the Boston Theatre, Sullivan was presented by his admirers with a diamond studded belt emblematic of the championship. This and his title were his two proudest possessions, and in the midst of his wild drinking and carousing, were the only considerations that could be urged to get him to sober up.

Another match was made between him and the slippery Charlie Mitchell, and the fight was held on the estate of Baron Rothschild at Chantilly, France, March 10th, 1888. Mitchell weighed only about 165 pounds, which was more than thirty pounds less than Sullivan, but he used his brains, his knowledge of London prize ring rules, and his legs. He jabbed and ran, over and over again. Sullivan caught him three times and knocked him down, but not out. It started to rain, and in the thirty-ninth round, as it was pouring heavily, the fight was called a draw. This gave Mitchell a great reputation for skill, but Sullivan retained the United States championship.

In the midst of a drinking spree in 1889, Sullivan was suddenly informed by Billy Muldoon that he was matched with Jake Kilrain, who had grown from a champion middle weight into a good heavy weight. Muldoon straightened Sullivan out and the fight took place August 8th, 1889, at Richbourg, Mississippi, near New Orleans. The time of year and the locality combined to make the day absolutely torrid. The encounter was with bare knuckles under London prize ring rules, and against the law, but could not be stopped by the sheriff.

Illegal as the contest was supposed to be, every few minutes the telegraph wires flashed its progress to the far ends of the country. The local operators informed the hotel and barber shop and poolroom, the newsboys on the trains relayed the reports to the passengers, and in short everybody within touch of the wires was kept informed about the fight.

In the first round Kilrain threw Sullivan, but was himself thrown to end the next round. The men fought on and on under the exhausting sun, but without doing any great harm to each other. Before the forty-third round Sullivan was given a mixture of whiskey and tea and it was said that the tea made him sick at his stomach. The fight went on interminably, both men weakened by the heat, but at last Sullivan was given the decision at the end of the seventy-fifth round.

This was the last championship fight with bare knuckles and under the old London rules. It began to be realized that it would pay better to promote open boxing exhibitions with gloves in the big cities under the Marquis of Queensbury rules than to pull off illegal bare-knuckle fights in spots sufficiently isolated to get away from the law.

Meantime, had Sullivan scanned the western horizon, he might have seen a small cloud no bigger than a man's hand arising, for in 1889 James J. Corbett, the good looking young bank clerk, knocked out Joe Choyinski in a fight with skin-tight gloves on a barge in San Francisco Bay. The fight went twenty-seven hectic rounds, and was won by a left hook, which, as a knock-out blow, was a new invention of Corbett's.

Lawn tennis in the eighties was nationally organized and started on an illustrious career. The first tournament that was open to any member of any club, was held by the Staten Island Cricket and Base Ball Club in September, 1880. O. E. Woodhouse, who had been runner-up to H. W. Lawford at Wimbledon that year, entered and won, astonishing all by an overhead service.

This tournament disclosed that the game was being played under different rules and with different balls in the various localities. In order to attain uniform conditions E. H. Outerbridge, of the Staten Island Base Ball and Cricket Club, Dr. James Dwight of the Beacon Park Athletic Association, and C. M. Clark of the All-Philadelphia Tennis Committee, called a meeting of clubs May 21st, 1881, which formed the United States National Lawn Tennis Association.

The first national tournament was played at Newport and won by Richard D. Sears. He stayed back when he served, but advanced to the service line when he thought he had a chance, and volleyed or smashed his opponent's drives or lobs.

In the doubles Sears and Dwight tried to play along the service line, but were beaten by C. M. Clark and F. W. Taylor, who played one up and one back, and who eventually won the tournament. By the next year Sears and Dwight had strengthened their volleying, and won the doubles championship, holding it in all five times.

In singles Sears continued to improve, and in 1884, after a trip to England, introduced a fast dropping drive modeled on but modified from H. W. Lawford's famous stroke. He won the championship seven times and retired undefeated.

Henry W. Slocum, who introduced the plan of returning his opponent's service deep to the baseline and following his shot to the net, won the championship in 1888 and repeated in 1889. The next year, however, he lost his crown to Oliver S. Campbell who originated the following of the service to the net, and who advanced the so-called center theory, which was that if he shot down the center it gave his opponent less chance for a pass as he rushed in.

During the decade lawn tennis was high in social favor. The championship tournaments were played in the Newport Casino, while in the summer resorts the game was the rage. Girls began to become proficient enough to play alongside of men in mixed doubles, and the game practically superseded croquet and archery as an outdoor social pastime.

A fashionable roller skating rink, 1880

A skating scene in Central Park, 1883

[225]

Bowling as a fashionable ladies' amusement, 1882

The ladies' class of the Fencers' Club, 1888

[226]

The first important tournament for women was held in 1883 by the Staten Island Ladies' Club for Outdoor Sports. In the final Miss Goodwin of the Franklin Archery and Tennis Club, New Jersey, defeated Miss Adelaide Robinson of Staten Island. Miss Goodwin, according to an eye-witness, played "up at the service line," and made "frequent and skillful use of the volley," but relied "more on placing than on force."

This tournament was not scheduled by the National Association, which did not "take the ladies under its protecting wing" until later, Miss Ellen F. Hansell in 1887 being the first official women's champion.

Such ladies' play, from the viewpoint of civilization, was particularly important, because lawn tennis was the first great sport or game for women developed in the country, and, though golf is a good second, probably the greatest for women that the world has ever known.

In the decade between 1880 and 1890, the pastimes in which women took an active part included particularly the lawn games of croquet, tennis, and archery, as already mentioned, but there are a few records of their participating in other sports.

Riding played an important part with a few, but was not an accomplishment acquired by any large percentage. It was practised on the bridle paths and exhibited at the hunts and the horse show. There were occasional ladies' equestrienne contests and races at the fairs. There is even an engraving of a woman on a high bicycle racing against a horse.

The beaches were gay with women, but not many of them really swam, though one woodcut illustrates a women's swimming race. Just as unusual is another print of a rowing race between women, though rowing or paddling was not so exceptional.

In rare instances they took part in sports in the mountains. An engraving depicts a woman shooting a deer in the Adirondacks, and another is of one fishing for trout with the assistance of a man.

Skating was still in vogue both on ice and on rollers. There are woodcuts of a women's fencing school, and several of women bowling, though this seems to have been more usual among the Germans.

[227]

Archery had pretty well disappeared as a social amusement when it was revived in the seventies by Maurice Thompson, who wrote *The Witchery of Archery* and promoted it at every opportunity. By 1879 there were at least twenty-five clubs in the country and a national tournament was held. For a decade or so archery was a recognized social pastime. In New York City in the eighties there were the Manhattan Archers, a hundred in number, who met at Mount Morris Park, 120th Street and Fifth Avenue, on Saturday afternoons, and the New York Archery Club which met at 88th Street and Eighth Avenue. Then there was a Brooklyn club in Prospect Park and another connected with the Ladies' Club for Outdoor Sports at New Brighton, Staten Island.

The usual uniform for men was a green coat, and a cap with a peak, with buttons or trimmings to denote the club. Ladies wore a jacket of similar green cloth and a white skirt. A good bow cost $6, a dozen arrows $11, bow strings a dollar each, a quiver $3, and an arm guard $2.

But though archery required skill and was interesting, it had to compete with the new game of tennis for favor, and while it involved rivalry in skill, it did not have the battle element of tennis, and largely for that reason did not maintain its standing as a nation-wide pastime.

While there are records of golf in the American Colonies as early as the eighteenth century, as previously noted, the modern development of golf here began in 1888. R. H. Lockhart, who had returned to Scotland, the land of his birth, became interested in golf there, and brought a supply of clubs and balls back with him to the United States.

He interested John Reid of Yonkers in the game, and they formed the St. Andrews Golf Club of Yonkers, which included John B. Upham, Harry O. Talmadge, Harry Holbrook, and Kingman Putnam, and laid out six holes near Reid's home. Like the original Wall Street brokers, they met at first under a tree in one corner of the grounds, but soon grew into a larger course and a clubhouse. They were followed in 1891 by the Shinnecock Hills Golf Club, and the game soon began to spread throughout the East, and here and there in the West.

The amateur lacrosse tournament at the Polo Grounds: the final game between the Yale and New York Clubs, 1883

A match game of polo between the New York and Jersey City teams at the Pavonia Rink, Jersey City, 1888

[229]

Patrol firing into a flock of geese in California, 1882

Hunting the prong-horn antelope in California, 1889

[230]

The significant points of golf were that it could be played by even one person, though far better by two or four, that it retained the interest by giving a chance for unlimited skill, that it was a game to be played rather than merely watched, and that the elderly and women as well as youths could play it. It did more toward getting grown men to play again, than any other sport had ever done. It required grounds larger than those of the cricket or polo club, and as it had to go into the country for them, it did more to establish country clubs than any other sport. While a few country clubs had been founded by fishing clubs and hunt clubs, golf carried the country club idea into every city of any size in the country.

This seems a logical place to pause in our history. It brings the subject up to a point within the memory of the present senior generation, and to what is in many ways a new era not only in American sport, but in American civilization.

LIST OF SOURCES

LIST OF SOURCES

This check list does not pretend to be exhaustive, but serves merely as a starting point for the student of American sporting literature.

KINGSBOROUGH, VISCOUNT; EDWARD KING
Antiquities of Mexico, 9 volumes.
London: 1831 - 1848.
Good for Aztec manuscripts.

CASTILLO, BERNAL DIAZ DEL
The True History of the Conquest of Mexico.
Translated from the Spanish of 1568.

MOTOLINIA, FRAY TORIBIO (Died 1568)
Historia de los Indios de la Nueva España.
Quoted in Clavijero.

ACOSTA, JOSÉ DE
Natural and Moral History of the Indies.
Translated from the Spanish edition of 1590.

CLAVIJERO, D. FRANCISCO JAVIERO
The History of Mexico.
Translated from the French of 1780.

LE MOYNE, JACQUES
Account of the French Expedition to Florida under Laudonniere, 1564.
Translated.

BRY, THEODORE DE
America.
Frankfort: 1590-1634.
In thirteen parts. (See specially parts 1, 2 and 10.)

CHAMPLAIN, SAMUEL DE
The Works.
Translated from the narratives of 1599-1618.

SMITH, CAPT. JOHN
Works, 1609-1621.

RECORDS OF THE NEW PLYMOUTH COLONY.
1620-1699.
Twelve volumes. Indexed.

MASSACHUSETTS BAY RECORDS.
1628-1674.
Four volumes. Indexed.

NEW YORK STATE DOCUMENTS RELATING TO COLONIAL HISTORY.
1603 — Revolution.
Fifteen volumes. Indexed.

RHODE ISLAND RECORDS.
1636-1792.
Ten volumes. Indexed.

MARYLAND ARCHIVES.
1637-1781.
Forty-seven volumes. Indexed.

DENTON, DANIEL
A Brief Description of New York.
London: 1670.

HENNEPIN, LOUIS
A New Discovery of a Great Country in America.
First English edition: 1698.

LAHONTAN, LOUIS, BARON DE
New Voyages to North America, 1683-1694.
Translated.

BOSTON NEWS-LETTER.
Boston: 1704-1763.

BEVERLY, ROBERT
History and Present State of Virginia.
London: 1705.

KNIGHT, MADAM SARAH KEMBLE
The Private Journal of a Journey from Boston to New York in 1704.

LIST OF SOURCES

CHARLEVOIX, PIERRE DE
> Journal of a Voyage to North America.
> *Translated. (See especially seventh letter, 1721.)*

BACQUEVILLE DE LA POTHERIE
> Histoire de l'Amérique Septentrionale.
> Paris: 1722.
> *Translated in part.*

JONES, HUGH
> The Present State of Virginia.
> London: 1724.

KALM, PEHR
> Travels into North America.
> *Translated from the Swedish edition of 1753.*

LE PAGE DU PRATZ
> The History of Louisiana.
> *Translated from the French edition of 1758.*

ACRELIUS, ISRAEL
> History of New Sweden.
> *Translated from the Swedish edition of 1759.*

ROYAL AMERICAN MAGAZINE.
> Boston: 1774.

BURNABY, REV. ANDREW
> Travels through the Middle Settlements.
> London: 1775.

ADAIR, JAMES
> The History of the American Indians.
> London: 1775.

CHASTELLUX, MARQUISE DE
> Travels in North America, 1780.

SPORTSMAN'S COMPANION.
> New York: 1783.

[237]

ANBURY, THOMAS
    Travels through the Interior Parts of America.
    London: 1789.

SPORTING MAGAZINE.
    London: 1792-1860.

CAMPBELL, PATRICK
    Travels in the Interior Inhabited Parts of North America.
    Edinburgh: 1793.

CITY GAZETTE AND DAILY ADVERTISER.
    Charleston, S. C.
    October, 1795.

LATROBE, B. H.
    Journal, 1796-1820.

CUSTIS, GEORGE W. PARKE
    Recollections and Private Memoirs of Washington.

BAILY, FRANCIS
    Journal of Travel in the Unsettled Parts of North America, 1796-97.

THE PORT FOLIO.
    Philadelphia: 1809-1820.

LEWIS AND CLARK EXPEDITION, 1804-1806.
    New York: 1814.

WILSON, ALEXANDER
    American Ornithology.
    Philadelphia: 1808-1814.
    Nine volumes.

CLARK, J. H., ATKINSON, ETC.
    Foreign Field Sports.
    London: 1819.

AMERICAN SHOOTER'S MANUAL.
    Philadelphia: 1827.

AMERICAN TURF REGISTER.
    1829-1844.

LIST OF SOURCES

CABINET OF NATURAL HISTORY AND AMERICAN RURAL SPORTS.
    Philadelphia: 1830-1832.

SPIRIT OF THE TIMES.
    New York: 1831, 1835-1890.

SMITH, JEROME VAN CROWNINSHIELD
    Natural History of the Fishes of Massachusetts.
    Boston: 1833.

IRVING, WASHINGTON
    Tour on the Prairies.
    Philadelphia: 1835.

CURRIER, N.
    Lithographs.
    New York: 1834-1857.

AUDUBON, JOHN JAMES
    The Birds of America.
    London: 1827-1838. Four volumes.
    New York: 1840-1844. Nine volumes.

WIED-NEUWIED, MAXIMILIAN, PRINZ VON
    Travels in the Interior of North America.
    Translated from the German edition of 1839-1841.

WILLIS, N. P.
    American Scenery.
    London: 1840.

TOWNSEND, J. K.
    Sporting Excursions in the Rocky Mountains.
    London: 1840.

HERBERT, H. W., "FRANK FORESTER"
    Articles in American Turf Register, 1839-; in the Spirit of the Times.
    The Warwick Woodlands.
    Philadelphia: 1845.

CATLIN, GEORGE
    North American Indians.
    London: 1841.

[239]

SCHREINER, W. H.
  Sporting Manual.
  Philadelphia: 1841.

NEW YORK ATLAS.
  New York: 1841-1858.

CASTELNAU, FRANCIS, COMTE DE
  L'Amerique du Nord.
  Paris: 1842.

THE ROVER.
  New York: 1843-1844.

HAWES, WM. P., "J. CYPRESS, JR."
  Sporting scenes.
  New York: 1842.

GRAHAM'S MAGAZINE.
  Philadelphia: 1841-1858.

FISHER, THOMAS
  Dial of the Seasons.
  Philadelphia: 1845.

LEVIGNE, SIR RICHARD GEORGE AUGUSTUS
  Echoes from the Backwoods.
  London: 1846.

ELLIOTT, WILLIAM
  Carolina Sports.
  Charleston: 1846.

BREEDER AND SPORTSMAN.
  San Francisco: 1847-1890.

HAWKER, PETER
  Instructions to Young Sportsmen.
  (Edited by "Frank Forester.")
  Philadelphia: 1846.
  Appendix on North America.

LIST OF SOURCES

HEADLEY, JOEL T.
   The Adirondacks.
   New York: 1849.

AGASSIZ, LOUIS
   Lake Superior.
   Boston: 1850.

PHELAN, MICHAEL
   Billiards without a Master.
   New York: 1850.

WEBBER, C. W.
   The Hunter Naturalist.
   Philadelphia: 1851.

ILLUSTRATED AMERICAN NEWS.
   New York: 1851-1852.

GLEASON'S PICTORIAL.
   Boston: 1851-1854.

ADVENTURES OF HUNTERS AND TRAVELLERS.
   Philadelphia: 1852.

KRIDER, J.
   Sporting Anecdotes.
   Philadelphia: 1853.

KENNEDY, JOHN P.
   The Blackwater Chronicle.
   New York: 1853.

THORPE, T. B.
   The Hive of "The Bee Hunter."
   New York: 1854.

HAMMOND, S. H.
   Hills, Lakes, and Trout Streams.
   New York: 1854.

GERSTAECKER, FREDERICK
   Wild Sports in the Far West.
   London: 1854.

LANMAN, C.
> Adventures in the Wilds of the United States.
> Philadelphia: 1856.

WEBB, W. E.
> Buffalo Land.
> Philadelphia: 1856.

LEWIS, E. J.
> American Sportsman.
> Philadelphia: 1857.

PALLISER, JOHN
> The Solitary Hunter.
> London: 1857.

LESLIE'S WEEKLY.
> New York: 1856-1890.

HARPER'S WEEKLY.
> New York: 1857-1890.

NEW YORK ILLUSTRATED NEWS.
> New York: 1859-1864.

CURRIER AND IVES.
> Lithographs.
> New York: 1857-1890.

WHITEHEAD, C. E.
> Wild Sports of the South.
> New York: 1860.

STREET, A. B.
> Woods and Waters.
> New York: 1860.

BERKELEY, G. C. G. F.
> The English Sportsman in the Western Prairie.
> New York: 1861.

HITTELL, THEODORE
> The Adventures of James Capen Adams.
> Boston: 1861.

LIST OF SOURCES

WRAXALL, Sir F. C. L.
    The Backwoodsman.
    London: 1864.

TURF, FIELD AND FARM.
    New York: 1865-1890.

CAPT. FLACK
    The Texas Rifle Hunter.
    London: 1866.

PEVERELLY, CHARLES A.
    Book of American Pastimes.
    New York: 1866.

TOWNSHEND, F. TRENCH
    Ten Thousand Miles of Travel, Sport, and Adventure.
    London: 1869.
    Wild Life in Florida.
    London: 1875.

ILLUMINATED WESTERN WORLD.
    New York: 1869.

MURRAY, W. H. H.
    Adventures in the Wilderness.
    Boston: 1869.

HARTLEY, C. B.
    Hunting Sports in the West.
    Philadelphia, 187-?

WARREN, THOMAS R.
    Shooting, Boating and Fishing for Young Sportsmen.
    New York: 1871.

GILLMORE, PARKER
    A Hunter's Adventures in the Great West.
    London: 1871.

DAILY GRAPHIC.
    New York: 1873-1889.

LIST OF SOURCES

FOREST AND STREAM.
New York: 1874-1890.

AMERICAN FIELD.
Chicago: 1874-1890.

NEW YORK SPORTSMAN.
New York: 1875-1890.

CARTWRIGHT, DAVID W.
Natural History . . . and Guide.
Toledo: 1875.

DODGE, R. I.
The Plains of the Great West and Their Inhabitants.
New York: 1877.

AMERICAN CRICKETER.
Philadelphia: 1877-1890.

CAMPION, J. S.
On the Frontier. Reminiscences of Wild Sports.
London: 1878.

THOMPSON, MARY E. DARTT
On the Plains and Among the Peaks.
Philadelphia: 1879.

BRENTANO'S MONTHLY.
New York: 1879-1880.

CROSS, D. W.
Fifty Years with the Gun and Rod.
Cleveland: 1880.

WILLIAMSON, A.
Sport and Photography in the Rocky Mountains.
Edinburgh: 1880.

NORTHRUP, A. J.
Camps and Tramps in the Adirondacks and Grayling Fishing in Northern Michigan.
Syracuse: 1880.

MURPHY, J. M.
   Sporting Adventures in the Far West.
   New York: 1880.

METROPOLITAN.
   New York: 1882-1883.

CYCLIST AND ATHLETE.
   New York: 1883.

AMERICAN ROLLER AND BASE BALL JOURNAL.
   Boston: 1885.

OUTING.
   New York: 1883-1890.